I Love My Church

But Oh

My God!

By
John Chuchman

This book was printed in
The United States of America by
Booksurge.com

Additional copies of this book
and copies of the author's other titles
"Springtime in Autumn,"
"Pebbles of Wisdom,"
"Quest,"
"Sunset Awakening," and
"Journeying Through Life"

may be ordered from Amazon.com
or from the author at

poetman@freeway.net
http://my.freeway.net/~poetman

Dedication

This book is dedicated

to all the faith-filled people
around the world

who care enough
about Church

to be willing to fight
to change it,

to help it grow

and become
more Christ-like

with a special Blessing

to all the members of
Voice of the Faithful (VOTF)
and especially
Call To Action (CTA).

Special Thanks to
Dear Friend Karen Schrauben
who helped in so many ways
to put this book together.

Introduction

In writing my poetry,
I never intended to focus
on the ills of today's Church.

Yet, my previous books
ended up containing expressions of
my sorrow with the Institution.

Church
has been an important part of my life
and my own spiritual growth
(although late in life)
has only served to amplify
the failings of the institution
(and its hierarchy).

This book
which contains a few thoughts
from my previous books,
as well as brand new ones,
is written in response to the requests
to publish a book, so focused.

Thus, "I Love My Church, but Oh My God!"

I care enough about My Church
to be willing to fight
to reform it,
to help make it more Christ-like.

I try to heed
the call of Pope John XXIII,
not to be a museum-keeper,

but instead,
one of God's gardeners,
tending the ever-changing,
ever-growing,

Gift of Creation

and

Church.

Submitted in Love,

John Chuchman

Why me?

I swore I'd never expend energies
trying to change
this mammoth institutional church.

Some may have been called
to do this,
but surely not me.
Let others try.

I vowed to spend my time and effort
helping the Bereaved
one on one, or in small support groups,
or in workshops or retreats.

I believed that I could help
keep the Tree that is church
healthy at the grass roots,
regardless of which red bird
is perched atop.

Yet why do I get so angry
at the un-Christlike activities
of this Institution?
Why do I spend so much energy
Writing letters to the Editors
And anybody else who will listen?

Why do I get so excited about
organizations like Call to Action and
Voice of the Faithful?

Are all the people
who bow when they're told, evil?
who pray as they're told, evil ?
who don't discuss
what they're told not to discuss,
evil?
who never grow beyond
conventional wisdom,
evil?

Of course not.

I get angry, not because they're evil,
but because they're missing so much.

And that so many of the hierarchy
want to keep them exactly so
angers me terribly.

Dear Holy Spirit, with Your help,
I go along and keep trying to help people
at the grass roots,
but aren't You just as angry
that this Institution has strayed so?

Dear Holy Spirit,

Please not me,

but Thee,

Unless, of course .

Great Expectations

Peace,
Perfection,
Wisdom,
Understanding,
Love,
Worry-free life.

Great expectations!

False expectations.

Perfect peace,
I am not promised;
The Holy Spirit simply liberates me from the
fear
of not having it.

From the human condition,
I am not redeemed;
The Holy Spirit simply gives me the strength
to
endure it.

A full understanding of life,
I am not awarded;
The Holy Spirit gives me
the courage to live it.

The love of others,
I am not guaranteed;
The Holy Spirit simple helps me to love
others
unconditionally.

From worry,
I am not freed;
The Holy Spirit simply gives me the wisdom
to
let the past go,
let the future be and
live in the precious present,

The Holy Spirit does not take me to a state
that is
trouble free;
She simply leads me through a life
lacking peace,
mired in imperfection,
affording no certainties,
providing no guarantees,
fraught with worry,

SAFELY.

The Creative Word of God
gives birth to the Blessing that is
Creation.

Humans bless other beings
in a conscious way
with creativity and compassion.

God is in us and we are in God.
Eternal Life is now;
no need to wait till death.

Spirituality is Cosmic, not introverted.

Letting go is
letting creation be the blessing it is.

Sink deeply into the ineffable depths of
the unfathomable ocean which is God.

We are sons and daughters of God and
need to let our limiting perspectives go.

Spirituality is a Growth Process.
Creativity is the work of God in us.

Compassion is the fullness
of Spiritual maturity.

11

Everyone is noble, royal, dignified and responsible for Justice and Compassion.

With His creativity and compassion, Jesus calls us to be God's Words and Children.

Spirituality is Laughter, Newness, Joy.

Faith

Not a set of dogmas
Not a set of beliefs
Not something cast in concrete never
changing
Not a code of conduct
Not a set of rituals
Not a credo
Not the port in the a storm
Not to pay, pray, obey

Faith is

Sailing the rough seas
Trusting God
Being comfortable in uncertainty
Willingness to Change
Awareness of the Guidance around us
Acceptance of what is
Letting go
Acting on Intuition

Loving Unconditionally

Eyes of the Heart

Some looked at lepers with disgust;
Jesus saw lonely humans,
crying out for acceptance.

Some looked at sinners with
condemnation;
Jesus saw wounded children of God
who could be saints.

Some saw Nathaniel as nothing special;
Jesus saw a man incapable of falsity.

Some saw Matthew as an idler;
Jesus saw a man awaiting a call.

Some looked at Zacchaeus as scoundrel;
Jesus saw a man ripe for conversion.

Some saw ordinary people as sinners;
Jesus saw sheep without a shepherd.

Some saw the widow in the temple as
a miserable woman
making a pathetic offering;
Jesus saw one making a heroic offering.

Some saw the thief on the cross
as a criminal;
Jesus saw a man longing for paradise.

The hierarchy of our church

sees gays as intrinsically disordered,

sees women as not worthy of ordination,

sees the divorced and remarried as sinners,

sees the laity as serfs in a feudal system,
unworthy of choosing priests and bishops,
unworthy of administering sacraments,
unworthy of preaching,
less than clergy,

sees the married as unworthy of
priesthood,

sees non-Catholics as lesser beings,
excluding them from the table,

sees priests and bishops as unaccountable.

Jesus understood
the leprosy of the leper,
the darkness of the blind,
the misery of those living for pleasure,
the poverty of the rich,
the thirst of the ordinary,
and the arrogance of
the self-righteous hierarchy.

Jesus saw with the eyes of heart.

When our hearts open,
Life begins;
When our hearts close,
Death begins.

Institutional church,
seeing without heart
is dying.

May we each and all
See with our eyes of heart

and
Re-form Church

in Christ's Image.

My Approach to Liturgy

I come in Thanksgiving
(for all my gifts)
offering my Apologies
(for not doing better with them.)

I experience Forgiveness
(for my shortcomings)
offering the only thing I have
of Value to God
(me.)

Imperfect as my gift is
(given the potential for perfection)
I know it is the only thing
God desires of me.

In giving myself,
I experience Acceptance
and in the process
God Blesses, Anoints, and Sanctifies me.

I am then sent forth
To share my Gifts with Others,
to Love
and to be Loved
in God's Name.

Like the bread,
I have been

Taken (chosen),
Broken,
Blessed,
and
Shared.

My Church

ONE, HOLY, CATHOLIC, APOSTOLIC

ONE
Not in structure, organization, culture, or practice,
But as Jesus, in Love and Forgiveness.

HOLY
Not in common external signs of piety,
But in the pursuit of internal Spiritual Growth.

CATHOLIC
Not as members of one universal organization,
But reaching out to serve ALL peoples of the world,
especially the marginalized.

APOSTOLIC
Not in physical lineage to the Apostles,
But living in the Holy Spirit as bestowed on them.

ONE, HOLY, CATHOLIC, APOSTOLIC
Not in a limiting or exclusive sense,
But in an Expanding and Inclusive sense.

Essential Messages of Vatican II

I

The Mission of Church
Is no longer to be exclusively focused on
preparing individuals
to attain eternal life;

But rather on
Witnessing to God's Love and Compassion
by bringing
Justice and Healing to the world
Here and Now.

II

Modernity
Is no longer viewed with
suspicion and antagonism

But rather with
Critical Sympathy
And
Engagement.
Church is to Share
The Joys, Hopes, Grief, and Anguish
of the age,
Rather than view them from afar.

Church now fosters
A Positive attitude towards
other branches of Christianity.

Church needs reform,
values Scripture,
heeds the Call of the Laity,
and
supports Collegial structures
in Church governance.

Prickly Apartness
Is
Dead.

. . . From the Constitution of the Church

. . . lay people have the obligation
to constantly develop
a more profound grasp
of their Christian faith.

. . . lay people need . . . spiritual goods
from the Church and from their pastors
to fulfill their call,
such goods are not only a privilege,
but a *right* as well.

In order to receive what they really need,
they must express their needs and wants
openly.

Lay people . . .
must play a part in providing leadership.

There are even times
when lay people have a *serious obligation*
to express their opinions and insights
about the Church.

Their wisdom and knowledge
often arise from valuable life experience.

Such wisdom
is to be *prized*
by Church leaders.

We Dissent/We Affirm

WHEREAS CHRIST'S LIFE AND CALL
WERE INCLUSIVE,
We Catholics dissent to the idea of an
exclusive church
and
We affirm an open and welcoming
catholic church.

WHEREAS CHRIST'S LIFE AND CALL
WERE FOR A UNIVERSAL CHURCH,
We dissent to a "Smaller-purer" Church
and
WE affirm CATHOLIC as universal.

WHEREAS CHRIST'S LIFE AND CALL
WERE NON-BUREAUCRATIC,
We dissent to hierarchical CONTROL
and
We affirm a church of free and open
discussion
Without fear.

WHEREAS CHRIST'S LIFE AND CALL
WERE FREEING,
We dissent to domination and fear and
We joyfully affirm Christ's gift of freedom.

WHEREAS CHRIST'S LIFE AND CALL
WERE TO LOVE,
We dissent to a love only of rules
and
We, as St. John, affirm that God is Love.

WHEREAS CHRIST'S LIFE AND CALL
WERE ANTI-ESTABLISHEMENT,
We dissent to the protection of
the status quo
and
We welcome change as an integral
aspect of creation.

WHEREAS CHRIST IS LEADER OF ALL PEOPLE,
we dissent to electing leaders in secret
by a few
and
We affirm transparency and accountability
and participation by all.

We dissent to the protection of the
institution
at any cost
and
We reaffirm our allegiance to Jesus Christ
His life and His message.

Spirituality

Spirituality is not solely
prayer and devotion
alongside my secular life.

Spirituality
refers to my entire life
as it is intentionally related to God.

My Spirituality
is the framework for
my believing life in the world.

My daily life
can no more be divorced from Spirituality
than my prayer from daily life.

Spirituality
is anchored in and validated by
the way I live.

My Spirituality
embraces and enjoys
my secular life.

The clergy live in the secular world
as much as I,
but their mission is to maintain
a worshipping community
where God's affirmation of the secular
is celebrated.

The clergy, thus, are not so much set apart
for sacred things,
as directed to a vitally important,
but *less central role*
in the mission of the church.

The primary characteristic of Spirituality
is
Freedom.

I was created,
as were ALL others,
to be unconditionally free in the world.

Being Free is common to All humans
and
is fundamental to our Spirituality.

We are created
with intelligence
and capable of deep feelings,
aware of our world.

We have a dynamism toward questioning,
exploring, and understanding.

We have the capacity for
problem solving, system building,
knowledge, and Wisdom.

The world is ours
to maintain,
to improve,
to save.

The baseline for Spirituality
is the world.
The Spiritual Project
is the world.

We are taken up with the world,
fully engaged in the world,
interested in things of the world.

I can and do affirm the higher reality of
God,
while trying to
live a life of integrity,
love,
build community,
and make the world a better place to be.

Though institutional religions
call us to rely on
external authorities,
hierarchy, scripture, etc.,
which are important sources of wisdom,
Freedom lies
in following the call of

The Holy Spirit

resident deep within each of us.

External authorities
only serve to trap us,

The Holy Spirit,

to Free us.

Beatitudes as Gifts, not Tasks

I am poor spirit
When I do not feel entitled,
When I do not feel in control,
When I see all I have as gift.

My Blessing: Gratefulness

I mourn my losses
When I sit in silence and weep
When I help bereaved find their way

My Blessing: Compassion

I am meek
When I challenge authority,
When I have no status to defend,
When I risk humiliation

My Blessing: Freedom

I hunger and thirst for justice
When I am deeply aware of needs of others,
When I respond to the needs of others

My Blessing: Profound Awareness

I am merciful
When I treat my injurer
better than they deserve,
When I act with kindness towards my offender

My Blessing: Kindness

I am pure of heart
When I see things as they are, not as I am,
When I see straight to the Heart of God

My Blessing: Vision

I am a peacemaker
When I know I am not right,
When I seek the truth of another,
When I know truth exists beyond what I know,
When I am willing to keep learning

My Blessing: Openness

I suffer persecution
When I am ridiculed for my ways,
When I am labeled a soft touch
for being poor in spirit,
When I am called too sensitive
for being a mourner,
When I am called a fool for being meek,
When I am called naïve for being merciful,
When I am called a heretic for being a
peacemaker
I am the Blessing.

A Priesthood

For nearly a thousand years
Our priests were not socially distinct
from us.

There were no seminaries;
One simply presented himself
three days before Ordination
for an oral exam.
If over 24 years old
with no physical defects,
and
a grasp of the Faith
and communication skills,
one was ordained
a priest.

Our priest was hardly distinguishable
from us.

Oh yes,
Our priests were more literate
than most of us,
but they had to work the fields
just as we.

Then in the middle ages,
the pontiffs
revamped priesthood
into a disciplined army
marching in-step
with the Pope,
set off from our "profane" occupations,
with special uniforms,
bent on ruling us,
a subservient laity.

We were then excluded from all
participation
With Mass becoming
the priest's business,
with us as spectators.

Altar garb set him apart,
and he whispered prayers
in a language we understood not.

We were separated from it
by a thick railing,
no longer allowed to bring up
ordinary bread for consecration.

No longer could we receive the bread in
our hands, standing up;
We were forced to kneel and receive it
on our tongues.

The Chalice was withheld.

And forced celibacy further set us apart.

And when the Protestants
embraced the Universal Priesthood,

The Catholic Church reacted
with reactive zeal
to further differentiate "our" priests
and all they did
was Sanctified even more.

The very foundations of Christianity
were said to rest on
a Sacred Priesthood.

And then Vatican II

And then the sex abuse scandal.

A discovery:

A view of the priest as Sacred
obscures or replaces
his status
as one of the baptized,
as another sinner, like us,
needing redemption.

A view of the priest as sacred obscures
his humanity.

We have made Baptism nothing
And
Ordination everything.

Church life is ultimately relational

A relationship between human laity
and
human priests
needs rebuilding.

Parishes need to be run
by priests and laity
In collaboration.

Church official
needs to stop painting
an iconic image or our priests.

Instead,
The new Vatican Instruction
which delineates the role of parish priests
tells us the priest
is in charge
by dint of his ordination
and
"father" to us all.

The "cultic" model of priest
espoused by the Vatican
will be
a tragedy for church.

Icons are beautiful
but brittle and fragile
and shatter with destructive results
(as we have seen).

A Priesthood of all believers
is the true call of Jesus.

Cultic priests are dominant at the moment;
But changing that forever
will be
a coming Priesthood of
Married Men and Women,

Us.

Bishops of the Catholic Church,

As Faithful Catholics,
We have a Right
To Your

Understanding and Empathy,
Decisiveness,
Correct Focus,
Persistence and Follow-through
Openness, and
Disclosure.

With the Sex-abuse of our youth
by priests of the Catholic Church,
You, instead, demonstrated

Naivety about the predators and their
crimes,
Insensitivity to the pain of the victims,
Disgraceful Indecisiveness in reporting
the crimes,
A shameful focus on protecting the
institution, not people,
No effort at establishing National policies
of protection,
Massive efforts to cover up the facts,
little effort to tell us
what happened and why.

Isn't it time
You stepped down
to give us

the Leadership we deserve.

Bishops' Prayer

Dear God,

Please forgive the Laity.

They actually had begun to think
the Liturgy was theirs.

They forgot that it is the clergy's
and that they are allowed to witness it
and participate
only in the way
we prescribe.

Forgive the common language,
Forgive the applause,
Forgive females at the altar,
Forgive the singing of popular songs,
Forgive the enculturation

of the liturgy entrusted to us your Bishops
by the Vatican.

Dear God,

Please forgive the Laity.

They actually had begun to think
that the group assembled at Liturgy
was part of the Eucharistic Consecration.

They forgot
that the consecration of bread and wine
requires a special power
given only to the ordained
by us Bishops
the only true successors to the Apostles.

Forgive them
for misunderstanding
Jesus' call to priesthood of the laity.

Dear God,
Help us to restore the liturgy
to what you intended.

Help us to make it
a Ceremony above and beyond and
apart from the laity,
one which they witness from afar
and attend in the prescribed manner.

Dear God,

Help us not slip back
to the times when the Church had no
professional clergy
and liturgy was celebrated in homes
by laity.

Help us return to the times

when clergy were deemed
Representatives of Christ
with special powers and honors

and Liturgy was celebrated
in one official language
in one official manner

as Jesus would have wished.

Dear God, please . . .

In the meantime,
we will undo all the harmful changes
since Vatican II
that have made liturgy so . . .

A Call

Move beyond being Roman.
Remain Catholic, but no longer Roman.
Tradition has no real energy.
Institutional church is engaged in
self idolatry
with little hope for true renewal and reform.
Do not hold off personal growth awaiting
institutional reform.

Embrace our historical sacramental
tradition of discovering the sacred
in the ordinary
with powerful objects, words and
movement,
powerful prayer and rituals.

Believe in a God present to us,
not distant "in the sky."
Embrace Jesus as one path to the sacred.
Believe that we each must find our path in
community to nurture and sustain us.

Jesus preached a Reign of God most
manifest in service to one another,
filled with healing for each and the world,
empowered by unconditional love.

This love leads us all to justice and peace.

Revelation is ongoing
and we are part of creating
the new revelation for all,
that the Reign of God calls us all to
freedom and justice and peace.

"Religion and Spirituality" are primarily
about how we live in community
so all can live in dignity
with justice and peace.
Religion is not about salvation and
saving our souls,
but freedom from all oppression,
freedom to embrace God's great love and
share it with all humanity.

Institutions, primarily religious institutions,
exist to help us discover the sacred
in the ordinary,
and live the life-giving holiness in family,
work and community.

Leave a suffocating institution to find
freedom and sacredness of life.

*Paraphrased from the Sharing
of a Dear Friend, Tim Schmaltz*

Some Questions

Isn't God both Mother and Father?

Isn't God as the Punitive Father a false god and an idol that serves empire-builders?

Isn't the notion of a punitive, all-male God, contrary to the full nature of the Godhead who is as much female and motherly as it is masculine and fatherly?

Isn't the idea that God is 'out there' or above and beyond the universe false? Aren't all things in God and

God in all things?

Isn't everyone born a mystic and a lover who experiences the unity of things and aren't all called to keep this mystic or lover of life alive?

Aren't all called to be prophets which is to interfere with injustice?

Isn't Wisdom Love of Life?

See the Book of Wisdom: "This is wisdom:

to love life" and

Christ in John's Gospel:

"I have come that you may have life and
have it in abundance."

Does not God love all of creation and
can't science help us more deeply
penetrate and appreciate the mysteries
and wisdom of God in creation? Is Science
no enemy of true religion?

Is Religion necessary? Or is spirituality?
Spirituality and religion

are not the same thing any more than
education and learning,

law and justice, or

commerce and stewardship

are the same thing?

Does Jesus call us to a new religion or to a
new life?

Spirituality is living life at a depth of
newness and gratitude,

courage and creativity,

trust and letting go,

compassion and justice.

Does not Jesus,

not unlike many spiritual teachers,

teach us that

we are sons and daughters of God and
are to act accordingly

by becoming instruments of

divine compassion?

Is not Sexuality sacred and

a spiritual experience,

a theophany (revelation of the Divine),

a mystical experience?

Is it not holy, deserving to be honored?

Isn't the priesthood all workers

(all who are doing good work are midwives
of grace and therefore priests) and

ought this priesthood be honored

as sacred and with workers

instructed in spirituality

in order to carry on their ministry
effectively?

Isn't Empire-building (in or out of church)
incompatible with Jesus' life and teaching
and with Paul's life and teaching and

with the teaching of holy religions?
Doesn't ideology endanger faith because
it replaces thinking with obedience, and
distracts from the responsibility of theology
to adapt the wisdom of the past

to today's needs?

Instead of theology doesn't it demand
loyalty oaths to the past?

Isn't Loyalty an insufficient criterion for
ecclesial office?

Aren't intelligence and

proven conscience needed?

Is The pope the church or

a ministry within the church?

Isn't Papalolotry

a contemporary form of idolatry

to be resisted by all believers?

Is creating a church of Sycophants

a holy thing?

Aren't sycophants

(Webster's dictionary defines them as
"servile self-seeking flatterers")

un-spiritual people,

for their only virtue is obedience?

Isn't a Society of Sycophants

— sycophant clergy, sycophant
seminarians, sycophant bishops,
sycophant cardinals, sycophant
religious orders of Opus Dei, Legionaires
of Christ and Communion and
Liberation, and the sycophant press—

unrepresentative of the teachings or

the person of the historical Jesus

who chose to stand up to power

rather than amassing it?

Aren't vows of pontifical secrecy

a certain way to corruption and cover-up
in the church as

in any human organization?

Isn't Original Sin

an ultimate expression of a punitive father
God and not a Biblical teaching.

Isn't Original Blessing (goodness and
grace) biblical?

Doesn't the term "original wound"

better describe the separation

humans experience on leaving the womb
and entering the world,

a world that is often unjust and
unwelcoming

than does the term "original sin?"

Aren't Fascism and

the compulsion to control

not the path of peace or

compassion with those who practice
fascism not fitting models for sainthood?

Isn't the seizing of the apparatus of
canonization to canonize fascists

a stain on the church?

Isn't dancing, whose root meaning in many indigenous cultures is the same as breath or spirit, a very ancient and appropriate form in which to pray?

Should not a diversity of interpretation of the Jesus event and the Christ experience altogether expected and

to be welcomed

as it was in the earliest days of the church?

Does unity of church mean conformity?

Is there not unity in diversity?

Coerced unity is not unity.

Isn't our connection with the earth

(first chakra) holy; and

our sexuality (second chakra) holy;

and our moral outrage (third chakra) holy; and our love that stands up to fear

(fourth chakra) holy;

and our prophetic voice

that speaks out holy (fifth chakra);

and our intuition and intelligence

(sixth chakra) holy;

and our gifts

we extend to the community of light
beings and ancestors (seventh chakra)
holy?
Does not the prejudice of rationalism and
left-brain located in the head

need to be balanced by attention

to the lower charkas

as equal places for wisdom and truth and
Spirit to act?

Is "Joy the human's noblest act?"
(Aquinas)

Is our culture and its professions, education
and religion, promoting joy?

Don't we experience God in experiences
of ecstasy, joy, wonder and delight?

Don't we experience God in darkness, chaos, nothingness, suffering, silence and in learning to let go and let be?

Don't we experience God in acts of creativity and co-creation?
Don't we experience God in our struggle for justice, healing, compassion and celebration?

Doesn't the Holy Spirit work through all cultures and all spiritual traditions and

blow "where it wills"

not the exclusive domain of any one tradition and never has been?

Doesn't God speak today as in the past through all religions and all cultures and

all faith traditions

none of which is perfect and

an exclusive avenue to truth

but all of which can learn from each other?

Isn't Deep Ecumenism a necessary part of
spiritual praxis and awareness in our time?
Since the "number one obstacle to
interfaith is a bad relationship

with one's own faith," (the Dalai Lama)

Isn't it important that Christians know their
own mystical and prophetic tradition,

one that is larger than a religion of empire
and its punitive father images of God?

Doesn't fourteen billion years of evolution
and unfolding of the universe

bespeak the intimate sacredness

of all that is?

Pedophilia is a terrible wrong

but isn't its cover-up by hierarchy

even more despicable?
Are loyalty and obedience ever a greater
virtue than conscience and justice?

Isn't a church that is more preoccupied
with sexual wrongs than with wrongs of
injustice itself sick?

Is homosexuality found among 464 species
and in 8 percent

of any given human population?

Aren't racism, sexism and militarism serious
sins?

Don't Seminaries as we know them, with
their excessive emphasis on left-brain work,
kill and corrupt

the mystical soul of the young

instead of encouraging the mysticism and
prophetic consciousness that is there?
Should they be replaced

by wisdom schools?

Isn't Inner work required of us all?

Should spiritual practices of meditation be
made available to all

to help in calming the reptilian brain?

Should silence or contemplation and learning to be still be taught to all children and adults?

Doesn't good outer work flow from

our inner work

just as action flows from non-action and true action from being?

Isn't the Dark Night of the Soul

a learning place of great depth?

Isn't stillness required?

Is Chaos a friend and a teacher and

an integral part or prelude to new birth?

Aren't the proper objects of the human heart truth and justice (Aquinas)

with all people having a right to these through healthy education and

healthy government?

Isn't "God" only one name

for the Divine One and

aren't there an infinite number of names
for God and Godhead and

still God "has no name and

will never be given a name?" (Eckhart)

Does not the grief in the human heart
need to be attended to by rituals and
practices that, when practiced,

will lessen anger and allow creativity to
flow anew?

Does not true intelligence include

feeling, sensitivity, beauty,

the gift of nourishment and humor which is
a gift of the Spirit,

with paradox, being its sister?

Gleaned from "A New Reformation"

By Matthew Fox

Catholic Education

Despite all the jocularity
about our grade-school education
by the good nuns,
I value all my Catholic Education;

St. Nicholas School
(Sisters of St. Basil the Great)
Weber High School (Resurrectionist Fathers)
John Carroll University (Jesuits) and
forty years later,
Saint Mary's University of Minnesota
(Christian Brothers)
Master of Arts in Pastoral Ministries.

And I'm still studying my religion daily.

I am convinced
Theology is an Adult Activity.

Unfortunately, Catholic Education
in Theology
begins at an age when students
can't comprehend it
and
usually ends at a time
when they could begin to understand it.

Many Adults are educated and Catholic,
but not Educated Catholics.

Some priests and bishops prefer it this way.
Just take a look at whom
Theology Education is focused
in parishes.

All of a sudden,

it dawned on me.
As a regular Sunday churchgoer and
contributor,
I thought I was mainstream Catholic.
Guess what.
I'm in the minority.

And all these years of regular church going
lulled me into the false notion
that by doing so and
contributing to the institution
I was being a "good" Catholic.

The majority of Catholics
had already discovered that
being a good Catholic
involves one heck of a lot more than
going to church regularly and
paying one's institutional homage.

They'd discovered
that it's all about how one lives
the message of Love Jesus preached—
even apart from churchgoing practices,
not even mentioned by Him.

I understand the reasons
the hierarchy places such a strong
emphasis on churchgoing and donating—
it pays their salaries.
But the real trap is
believing that it is the essence of our Faith.

It not only is not,
but it can become one's
modern day golden calf, church as idol.

Perhaps Jesus' second coming
will involve the destruction of
today's temple
just as His first coming foretold
its initial destruction.
Do bankruptcies presage it?

It seems many Catholics
have turned to small faith groups and
home liturgies
in disgust over the many sins of
a bureaucratic, hierarchical, non-inclusive,
self-serving chauvinistic organization.

Perhaps these people
are the true traditionalists,
returning to Catholicism's earliest roots

rather than the way it was
when we grew up.

The institution's existence
has depended on making us all
dependent on IT
rather than the call of the Holy Spirit within.

There aren't too many people any more
who can be led into that bushel and
kept there—at least for very long.

I suspect
I'll continue to be a regular churchgoer
even though none of my children are
but I will try to direct my donations of
time, talent, and treasure to the needy,
the truly needy.

Celebrate

Are we celebrating

The shortest day?
The end of darkness?
The lengthening daylight?

Enlightenment?
Hope for a better future?
The beginning of Winter?

Change?
Rebirth?

Giving? Receiving?

Birth of an historical Jesus?
Birth of a Jesus-Attitude in us?

Incarnation?
Ours?
God's?

Hard to discern just exactly what It is

We are Celebrating.

Checking out churches

OTHER THAN tradition,
there is no clear reason
why religious organizations
should be exempt from
the duty to disclose financial information
required of other nonprofit charities.

We need a law
to help to bring religious groups
into the modern era of
financial accountability.

The need,
is rooted in the struggles of Catholic
parishioners to glean financial
information from the hierarchy
during the church's ongoing, controversial
efforts to close parishes.

Donors, parishioners, and neighbors of any
congregation,
regardless of denomination,
would benefit from the requirements for
greater transparency.

Let's require every charitable organization,
both religious and secular,
to list each piece of real property it owns
as part of its annual financial report.

Currently, such information is scattered
in property registries across the states,
often under real estate trusts.

Nonprofit organizations
other than religious organizations
are required to provide annual reports of
basic financial data, such as top salaries,
fund balances, and
gross revenues and expenses.

That is a small price to ask
in return for freedom from property taxes,
as well as state sales tax exemptions,
special mailing rates, and other privileges.

Donors to educational,
medical, and social service charities
use financial disclosures to
track fundraising efforts and
protect against waste and fraud.

Contributors to religious organizations
are just as deserving of
such protections.
But they are left in the dark.

Financial accountability
Is another way to have
moral accountability.

It is likely that opponents of a bill
will perceive it as an assault on
the church-state wall of separation.

But it is hard to see how a requirement
to disclose basic financial records
amounts to a constitutional violation.
The bill would apply
equally to all denominations.
And the bill poses no obvious threat of
state entanglement with religious beliefs.

All charities,
including religious organizations,
were required to report
financial information and property holdings
in the 1930s and '40s,
though enforcement was lacking.

Churches used their
unquestioned clout in 1954
to exempt themselves from the law,
creating today's two-tier system of
financial disclosure.

We now has an opportunity to
serve believers
with financial accountability.

Call your legislators.

Church

If we choose to believe

that in choosing the twelve
from among all the disciples,

Jesus intended to create
a *structured* community,

we do not have to believe
that the community exists
only when the structure exists.

The coming into being
of Church

was/is a *dynamic* process,
likely gestating in Jesus' mind,
not fully developed at His death,

not fixed for eternity,

and ever changing

in response to the movement of

The Holy Spirit.

Church and Change

Change for Christians
implies
Conversion,
Metanoia,
becoming New.

It calls us
to an Openness
to the Spirit
Who reveals Herself
in unexpected ways.

As affirmed in Vatican II,
We are Pilgrim Church
Always on the Move.

The Role of Church
is to bring about
Change in the World;

Change for Justice,
Change for Peace,
Change for Human Dignity,
Change for Freedom.

Church must be
the Agent of Change.

Only as such can it be a Servant of God.

Church Theology
Becomes
Obsolete
Irrelevant

if it is not Re-Expressed
in the context of today's Reality.

Church, itself
becomes
Obsolete,
Irrelevant
if it is
Set in Stone.

The Word of God
is Living,
Life-Giving.
It must be
Re-Interpreted
in terms of our understanding of life today,
in terms of current scholarship.

The Church does not
Have
God
or
Grace
or
Truth,
But only is
Growing into them.

Our primary obstacle is Fear:

Fear to let go,
Fear of Unknown,
Fear of Failure,
Fear of Loss,
Fear of Alienation,

Fear of Change.

God is present in All.

Fear lacks trust that God is in our Future.

Communicating with Bishops

The Catholic Church's structure
is hierarchical
by design.
All power flows down from the top.
All real power resides in specific individuals
and not in collegiate groups or structures.

This has been the case
throughout the history of
institutionalized Catholicism.

This structure has created a culture
surrounding the leadership.
This culture has produced
pre-conditioned responses
to different forms of communication.

The hierarchical governmental has given
rise to two things:

First,
The way authority is exercised.
The style is monarchical;
The focus is on the leader,
not on the subjects.

Second,
The ascendance of an aristocracy
composed of the clergy.
Power, privilege, prestige and
financial control
are vested in individuals
and all of these are members of the clergy.

Though lay persons have been included on
many levels of church administration,
all real power
is in the hands of a small group
of celibate, male clerics.
The real power is limited to
a select group of clerics,
the bishops.

In 1906 Pius X issued an encyclical
describing the structure of the Catholic
Church:

*THIS CHURCH IS IN ESSENCE
AN UNEQUAL SOCIETY,
THAT IS TO SAY A SOCIETY COMPRISING
TWO CATEGORIES OF PERSONS,
THE SHEPHERD AND THE
FLOCK....*

*THESE CATEGORIES ARE SO DISTINCT
THAT THE RIGHT AND AUTHORITY
NECESSARY FOR PROMOTING AND
GUIDING ALL THE MEMBERS
TOWARD THE GOAL OF SOCIETY
RESIDE ONLY IN THE PASTORAL BODY;*

*AS TO THE MULTITUDE,
ITS SOLE DUTY
IS THAT OF ALLOWING ITSELF TO BE LED
AND OF FOLLOWING ITS PASTORS
AS A DOCILE FLOCK.*

There is no indication from the writings of
the first three centuries
that Christ ever intended to found a
church as such
nor that he consciously established a
hierarchical system.

The Apostles emerged
from the Last Supper
as potential leaders of the future "church"
though they hardly knew it at the time.

That they emerged as archbishops,
newly ordained by Christ the High Priest
is Catholic mythology
but not an essential and proven element
of authentic ecclesiology.

The Catholic Church rests on a
sacramental system.
The seven sacraments are the particularly
important if not essential
Encounters with Christ.

Belief in the official theology of the
sacraments is essential for a Catholic.
The sacraments are necessary for
salvation, as we are taught.
The way to the sacraments is through the
ordained clergy,
especially the priests
but ultimately the custodians of the
sacraments
are the bishops.

Catholics learn early on
that salvation is mediated
through the Church
but not the Church as a vast throng of
believers scattered throughout the world.
It is mediated through the Church's
ordained leaders.
These leaders determine
who may receive a sacrament.
They control access to
the means of salvation and
as such, they hold great power
which supports the respect
in which they are held and
enables also the fear experienced
by so many Catholics.

The obvious power imbalance
determines the quality of communications
with the hierarchy
and the hierarchy's belief in its divine origin
formed the emotional response
to any communications that were critical
or challenging.

Often, rather than respond to the
substance of a criticism
or challenging question,
a bishop reacts defensively,
asking how his authority
can possibly be questioned.
The fundamental issue is lost
in the perceived threat
to the bishop's authority.

This attitude is enforced
by the church's own political structures
which reserve all power to bishops
and limit the participation of collegiate
bodies to consultation.

The clergy sex abuse phenomenon
has changed the way Catholics
communicate with bishops.
Accustomed to always controlling
every situation,
the bishops have reluctantly learned
that this is no longer the case.

Since the canonical structures
of the Church
provide no basis or avenues for
communication based on the concept of
equality of participants,
the aggrieved have sought relief
in the civil courts.
The bishops were faced with a power
equal to and in many ways surpassing
their own.
The result has generally been
defensiveness,
de-valuation of the abuse survivors, and
anger.

The frustration and anger
engendered in tens of thousands
of sex abuse victims
as well as millions of laity
over the sordid revelations
of abuse and cover-up
has changed the way
a significant segment of the Catholic and
non-Catholic population
communicates with bishops.

As the "scandal" unfolded
and more and more was revealed
in the media and in the courts,
trust and respect for bishops
rapidly eroded
and with it the traditional belief
in the nature of the episcopacy.

Communication has been challenging,
confrontative and
driven by anger, distrust and cynicism.
Those directly involved
with the sex abuse phenomenon,
including victims, their loved ones and
supporters,
the media and attorneys,
have been astonished, disappointed and
saddened
by the arrogance, dishonesty and
lack of compassion
manifested by many bishops.

The bishops realized that they have lost the
trust and respect of many.
Yet the fundamental attitude of superiority
still permeates most conversations
about significant issues facing
the Catholic Church.

The anger and mistrust has prevented true
communication.
Many bishops have immediately focused
on the challenge to their authority
rather than the reason for the anger.

The horror of the sexual abuse
of countless children, minors and
vulnerable adults
has been overshadowed for many bishops,
by the affront to their dignity,
the rejection of their authority
and the disrespect for their persons and
their office.

Most of the anger experienced by the
victims, their supporters
and others seeking reform and change
is grounded in the enormity of the crimes
and the perceived inability
of many bishops
to fully realize the gravity of the situation.

They have reason to be angry and
disrespectful of bishops.
As many have said time after time,
"They just don't get it."
"They think its all about them."

The welfare of the victims
should be the primary concern
of the institutional Church
because these men and women,
boys and girls,
have not only had their bodies and their
emotions deeply scarred,
but their souls devastated.

For a Church whose ultimate and
foundational mission
is the "salvation of souls"
there seems to have been precious little
concern
for the souls of those faithful and
trusting Catholics
who were raped and brutalized by priests
and bishops.

Why has the image of the institutional
Church's leadership been more important
than the spiritual and emotional welfare
of the tens of thousands
of clergy abuse victims.

To these questions
there have been no answers.
There has only been more equivocation,
more diversionary tactics and
more arrogance.

The body of bishops remains defensive
and aloof.
The good will and efforts
Of those who truly "get it"
are hidden by the intransigence
of those who continue to focus on
themselves,
trapped in a narcissistic self-image
that serves as a barrier to true insight
and authentic pastoral compassion.

We lay people must forge
the new set of rules
for communicating with the hierarchs.

We lay people always deferred to the
bishops
and generally believed
that their assessments, conclusions and
action plans
were always right.
This was almost always true
in direct dealings with bishops.

Out of earshot however, some lay persons
often expressed disagreement,
disappointment or even anger
at bishops and their actions.
Yet none would ever confront or forcibly
question them.
That simply wasn't done.
They were, after all,
the divinely appointed successors
of the apostles.

Bishops who refuse to include lay people
on every level of discussion and
decision making
must be confronted
and, in a rational, firm
yet respectful manner,
asked to explain such an exclusion.

There is no longer room for fear, secrecy or
arrogance.
Far too much is at stake
and far too many souls
have been devastated.

It is possible to confront the contradictions
between the spirit of Vatican II
and spirit of clerical mistrust.

In doing so it is
essential to understand the clerical context
from which the opposition arises.
The bishop is essential to the institutional
structure of the Church.

The theological and structural tradition
teaches that the church is founded
on the bishops
who are therefore essential
for its very existence.
The chain of authority in the three-fold
office of the bishop
is believed to be
the divinely directed means
whereby God communicates with mortals.

Consequently, challenges to bishops
are perceived as much more than
personal attacks
or manifestations of disrespect.
Such challenges
are expressions of disbelief
in an essential tenet of faith.

On the other side,
those who challenge the bishops'
autocratic exercise of authority
do not see such challenges as an affront to
a doctrinal issue.
Rather they see them as a reaction
to the reality of authority either misused
or abused.
The bishops see themselves as divinely
appointed leaders
while their critics see them
as flawed administrators.

The differences are not solely about power.
The differences
are about a variety of issues
that is far more serious
than ownership of power.

Soul murder, rape, sexual assault,
character assassination,
slander and financial mismanagement are
some of the known abuses
That many are up in arms about.

These issues will not go away
nor will they be rectified unless drastic
attitudinal changes take place,
primarily on the part of
the church's leadership.

Building bridges and opening lines
of true communication
between the bishops and lay people
is a noble goal
for members of the Christian community
but it will never happen
without integrity and trust.

Trust will not happen
until the traditional secrecy
and its sibling, fear, are eradicated.

Lay people should not fear
honest confrontation
with bishops or other church leaders.

This is an essential step
in the search for truth and accountability.
Banishing the fear that always lurked
in the background
is the beginning of
authentic Christian empowerment.

Searching for plausible answers
does not equal disrespect
nor is it a sign of dissent.

Above all
it is a sign that one has accepted
the sometimes painful and
challenging responsibility
of adult membership in the Body of Christ.

Confrontation need not equal fanaticism.
Working together begins with dialogue
and dialogue cannot begin
with capitulation.
Lay persons have been nurtured
by an ecclesial culture
that made true dialogue impossible.

The duplicity revealed by
the sex abuse scandal
led to the subsequent erosion
of trust and respect for clerics
and especially bishops.
This will be reversed
when both sides move beyond roles
and see one another as Christians.

This will be much more difficult for bishops
but this does not mean
that lay men and women
can or should retreat
to mindless deference.

Authentic dialogue is essential and
possible.
This means calling the issues in truth.

Confrontation does not mean
irrational anger
nor can it be productive if
minds and hearts are closed
to the possibility of good will.

**Gleaned from an article by
Thomas P. Doyle, O.P., J.C.D.
April 13, 2005 with his permission**

Content or Container

So many Catholics,
including hierarchy,

seem obsessed with the forms and format
of their religion,
(kneeling, standing, sitting, right words, etc)
rather than
its Content,

As Richard Rohr says,
substituting Church-ianity for Christianity.

Those addicted to issues of format,
loving the container
while missing the Content,
may look upon those
Living the Content of Jesus' message
(Inclusiveness, Love, Compassion,
Forgiveness)
with
Awe and Inspiration

But many will view
those trying to Live the Content
In any format
as being

dangerous, heretical, sinful, and
unorthodox,
just as they did

Jesus.

Contrasts

Narrow Religion

seeks to fortify and separate.

Deep Religion

seeks to Transcend.

Deep Religion

seeks to disclose Truth of the Cosmos.

Deep Religion

involves higher levels of human
development.

Deep Religion
involves the direct investigation
of experiential evidence disclosed
in higher stages of consciousness.

Dominator hierarchies
are rigid social hierarchies
that are instruments of oppression.

Actualization hierarchies

are growth hierarchies
seek the self-actualization of the
individuals.

Narrow Religion

refers to mental beliefs.

Deep Religion

refers to the higher trans-personal realms
beyond mere beliefs.

Dear Catholics,

It is with the deepest sorrow that we apologize for the performance of the church hierarchy over the past years.

It is terribly unfortunate that we have totally lost sight of the Mission of Jesus Christ and instead made perpetuating the institution—and our jobs in it—our prime mission.

Jesus' life and message were non-bureaucratic, inclusive, and disruptive, and we have been none of these.

We see no easy way to apologize for or correct this situation within the established framework, so we are taking a more revolutionary approach.
We are disbanding, dissolving, eliminating, the hierarchy and the hierarchical structure of the Church.

Its monarchical, feudal structure is obsolete and long outdated anyway.
We are turning over any and all parishes to you.

You elect and appoint your priests
from among you,
re-appointing existing ones only if you wish.

Of course, you may select from
ANY of your Faith Family, single or married,
male, or female.
You decide.

If you feel that having a Bishop would be
useful, elect one.

Celebrate Christ's Liturgy as best fits your
needs and culture
consecrating your meal as a Community
Gathered in the Holy Spirit.

We urge you to seek each others'
forgiveness and to forgive each other as
Jesus did.
And we ask you to forgive us
for our serious sins.

Baptize in Christ's name, Confirm in the
Holy Spirit, Bless Marriages and
those divorcing as well.

Anoint the sick and dying and
Love all fully.

Spread the good news of God's love for all
throughout the world and feel free
to use any resources in Rome—
but only as you wish.

We are deeply sorry for our abuse
of your trust, for abusing children, and
for misusing the hard-earned funds
you donated to further our own needs and
power.
Please forgive us.

All titled clergy are being sent home
immediately to face and live with
the people of God.

Love,

Pope, Cardinals, Bishops, etc.

Discovery/Confession

I've been critical of

conservative Catholics

for being museum keepers

and

for being frozen in the past

when

I discover that,

in my futile efforts to help reform Church,

I am just as guilty,

by my letting the Institution define
Catholicism for me,

rather than

Jesus Christ.

Jesus was not bound by the hierarchy of
His time,

why have I been letting the hierarchy of
my time

contain my idea of

True Catholicism.

Jesus' life and message were

inclusive, disruptive, and non-bureaucratic;

Did I really think

the Institution of today

could be the same?

Ecumenism

We seek progress
with regards to ecumenism
by celebrating joint Last Supper services.

We faithful may simply have to solve
the ecclesial prohibition
to celebrate joint Last Supper services
on our own
just like the question of birth control,
always under the auspices of
conscience.

The more pastors will decide to
celebrate joint services,
the more things will change.
There should be no parish
which will not discuss this.
We are not willing to wait
another 30 years.

If we faithful were able to vote
by a show of hands
or through signatures,
the problem would have long
been solved.

The questions of ecclesial ecumenism
have long been solved theologically,
now all that needs to be done is apply
this in practice.

However, here the Vatican's
consciousness of power is the problem.
Here the authoritative standing
of the Church
is definitely supposed to be kept in tact,
and that's why they're playing
power games
with the Eucharist.

This really has nothing to do with Jesus
anymore.
If Jesus could be here today
and see the churches
with their power structures and dogmas
exclude each other
from the Lord's Supper,
which He instituted,
He would banish the fanatics
as he banished the money changers
from the temple.

Does this unity not mean that we will
have to give up our own identity?

Not at all,
the future of ecumenism
is going to be like osmosis.
No one has to be scared
that he will have to accept
the infallible Pope.
No one will have to do without
the Eucharist.

But the real question is much broader:
how can Christendom,
how can the Pope,
advocate world peace,
advocate dialogue with Islam,
if it's not even possible to come to terms
with each other
and find a solution to such a problem?
The churches make themselves
incredulous this way.

Just where are women in the church?
Isn't God actually female?
This question, too will be solved
by practice,
simply because there will not
be enough male celibate priests.

To: **All the parishioners of churches facing closure in next five years**

Dearest Parishioners:
As an alternative to the closing of your
parish church because of a lack of
ordained celibate male priests,
we offer the following:

With prayer and in humility, nominate from
among your ranks a team of people—
single or married, male or female—
with the following skills, talents, interests,
and aspirations: Administration, Finance
and Accounting, Spirituality, Adult
Education, Youth Ministry and Education,
Management, Music, Liturgy, Facility
Management, and Caregiving and
Counseling.

Those you select may or may not be
presently employed by your parish.
We know there are many
amongst your number
that have earned advanced degrees
in their fields—including Religion—and
benefited from many years of outstanding
experience and we encourage you to
count them among your nominees.

Once you have nominated
your parish team,
we offer to train them
to be Your Leaders of Your Local Church.
Furthermore, in order that you have full
access to the Sacraments, we will prepare
your team to Celebrate
all the needed Sacraments with you.
We will also train them to celebrate the
Sacred Liturgy with you.

Pray and call on the Holy Spirit to help you
find the talent, skills, interest, and
dedication
needed to lead your parish;
we vow to help those you choose
lead your parish and
to keep it from closing.

In view of your Faith,
this is the least we can do;
and it is as Jesus did and
would have us do.

With Love and Appreciation,
Your enlightened Hierarchy and Pope

Eucharist as Communion

Eucharist
is supposed to have a Transforming effect
on us.

Eucharist is supposed to send us forth
determined to do something.

Eucharist is supposed to
change our priorities.

Many prefer a docile, consoling Eucharist.

Many see it as a product
for personal consumption.

John Paul II proclaimed that
Eucharist fosters Social Love,
seeking Common Good
over private food.

And yet,
Vatican pronouncements
and upcoming documents
concentrate on

Eucharist as object of adoration.

The Vatican approach
is one-sided, discouraging, and
totally inadequate.

"The Eucharist:
Source and Summit
of the Life and Mission of the Church"
is preoccupied with

ceremonial propriety.

The Vatican
overemphasizes adoration
vs. Service

and an individualistic link
between believer and Jesus.

Lost by the Vatican
is St. Augustine's plea
to partake of Christ's body
to become Christ's body in the world.

Lost by the Vatican
is the intimate connection
between Eucharist
and Service.

Dioceses
are promoting Eucharistic adoration
as never before.

A few churches
expose the Eucharist sparingly
because their pastors
want parishioners to see
that THEY are tabernacles of Christ.

The Vatican emphasis
tends to provide people
a place to hide
from the cares of the world.

Once again,
the Vatican
is out of touch
with the real world,
and
has got it wrong.

Eucharist IS Communion.

Freedom

Jesus gifted us with Freedom.

As He stated in His Sermon on the Mount,
Through Love,
We can be free from

worldly securities,
the need for constant pleasure,
power, control and approval,
conventional wisdom,
over-identification with a group,
our hurts,
lack of forgiveness,
our minds,
results,
and self possessiveness.

Yet, Institutions
even Church
try and take away
these Christ-given gifts.

They encourage us to

find Security outside ourselves, in them,
relinquish power and control to them,
rely on their wisdom,
identify totally with them,
seek forgiveness through them,
keep it mental,
but not think for ourselves.

Who gave these institutions the right
to take away

our Gift of Freedom?

What made us so weak-kneed
to relinquish

our Gift of Freedom?

Freedom and Spirituality

The Freedom of the Children of God
proclaimed by the Gospel in many ways
is today being transgressed
within our community of faithful itself.

Oh, the Laity of the Church are active,
but to be active
and to be Free
are not the same.

The Laity, for the most part,
do not know of their oppression,
and would deny it
if argued in their presence.

The worst form of oppression,
Spiritual,
is one in which
the captives have been induced
to embrace their own oppression.

This structural oppression
limits the freedom of
the entire Faith Community,
including the leadership,
who find it the hardest
to think outside the box.

This is not about Laity vs. Clergy.

The structural changes
required of Church
come best from below,
from those are least invested
in
maintenance of
the present structure.

Gift?

Growing up

in the Church
and
Church Schools,

I was given a Great Gift
of my
Catholic Education.

I memorized it all,
the prayers,
the answers to all worldly challenges,
"fear" of God,
the "truths"
feeling comfy
that my religion was the One True Religion
and that all others
were in serious risk of
eternal damnation.

Only years later
did I recognize that trap
that had been set for me.

Those "running" the church
never wanted any of us

to move beyond the
boundaries set for us,

to move beyond
conventional wisdom,

to challenge
hierarchical pronouncements,

to grow.

The gifts given me as a child
entrapped me as an adult
if I dared not
ask, seek, question, and challenge.

Hope to Women in the Church

The Document
The Church in the Modern World
(Gaudium et Spes)
from
Vatican II

provides Hope for
all Women in the Church.

Its message is grounded in
the Inalienable Dignity
of the Human Person
created in the Image of God.

Human Dignity, Freedom, Community,
Equality of All Persons, and Social Justice
are all rooted in
Man and Woman created in God's image.

It sees the Church
at the Service of Humanity.

Women are called,
not just to serve the family,
but to Service of the world.

It encourages Dialogue.

113

It is vital for the world
and greatly desired by the Church
that the two meet,
get to know each other,
and Love one another.
(Pope Paul VI)

Gaudium et Spes
called all Men and Women
to see oneself as God's image,
as Servants of the world,
and Partners in Dialogue.

Is it any wonder
those males who wish to keep control
would bury Gadium et Spes
and all of Vatican II with it.

Only Heroes

Noah, Abraham, Jacob, Joseph,
Moses, David, etc.
the heroes, the good guys.

Eve Delilah, Jezebel, etc.
evil women?

No heroines?

Shiprah and Puah and Miriam,
Even the Pharaoh's daughter,
saved Moses from death.

Rehab of Jericho,
despite being labeled a harlot
was instrumental in bringing the city down.

Hanna's strength and persistence and
courage,
brought forth Samuel,
one of the great prophets and judges.

Ruth's love and faithfulness and courage
Brought forth a great great grandson,
King David.

Judith and her maid
saved all Israel from the Holofernes.

Queen Esther,
despite her timidity,
delivered Israel from harm.
The little Hebrew girl,
slave of Naaman,
helped cure his leprosy
and win her freedom.

Mary and Elizabeth
kick-started Christianity.

Hildegard of Bingen, Clare of Assisi,
Julian of Norwich,
Catherine of Siena, Teresa of Avila,
Therese of Lisieux,
Mary Magdalene, etc., etc., etc.

Do we lack heroines?

Only in the telling.

(But, then, who are the storytellers?)

A dysfunction?

A hierarchy
whose identity comes from power
and patriarchy,
not relationships and intimacy,
Imposing celibacy on its operatives
Without adequate support

resulting either in

Sexual addiction
or
Sexual anorexia

barely bearable when viewed as
A charism of service to church,

Unbearable when imposed
by
A hierarchy
Not needing relationship and intimacy.

Church Awry

Why does the principle of subsidiarity,
an essential element
of Catholic Social Teaching,
take a back seat to
The Institution's need to perpetuate itself?

Why is Class Struggle by the poor,
with whom the Catholic Church espouses
solidarity,
often ignored or condemned
so the Institution can protect
internal cohesion.

Why is human dignity,
a cornerstone of Catholic Teaching,
abused and contradicted with action

by the need to protect
Institutional Authority?

Why is solidarity with the poor,
the stated preference
of the Catholic Church,
overwhelmed by bishops' penchant for the
affluent and powerful
In order to protect
the Institution's economic base?

Why are Freedom of Religion
and Primacy of Conscience,
boldly proclaimed
as Catholic fundamentals,
offered only to non-Catholics
In order to maintain Institutional Order?

Why is Non-Discrimination and
Inclusiveness,
as exampled by Jesus Christ,
only Selectively applied by an all-male
celibate hierarchy

To maintain
an all-male celibate controlled
Institution?

Why is the Good News
we are commissioned to spread
made subservient
to maintenance of the Institution
established to spread it?

Evangelize or Not?

It seems to me:

the Religions of the world
affirm an Ultimate Reality,
which they conceive and name
in different ways
and which
transcend the material universe
and is immanent within it.

While this Ultimate Reality
is beyond the scope
of complete human understanding,
many seemed to have experienced
Its Presence
in diverse ways
some of which have given rise
to the world's religions.

The world's great Religions,
including their different
and sometimes incompatible teachings,
offer authentic paths to
The Supreme Good.

The world's religions
share many basic values,
such as
Love, Compassion, Justice, and Honesty.
Some religions are misused
for purposes
contrary to the core values.

Each person
must follow his/her own conscience;
the possibility of conversion
is part of a human right
to religious freedom.

Traditional assertions
of exclusive possession of
absolute truth
repel people
who seek the Wisdom
that other religions offer.

Major efforts
on the part of one religion
to convert those of another religion
to their beliefs
may be misdirected.

Dialogue among peoples
of different religions
who wish to learn and benefit
from another's inheritance and insights,

and not evangelization,

should be the driving force
for relationships among peoples.

There is a need
to heal historic antagonisms
between people of different religions.

Let it begin with me.

Magesterium

Bishops and Cardinals,
miters and flowing robes,
power and majesty,
demanding reverence

The Irreverent Incarnation,
God's own gesture of irreverence

Pundits and prudes, and a Magesterium
would deem a Grand Entrance
by the Messiah
more appropriate than
an appearance by a crying, puking babe,

an Irreverence by a God
who resolutely chose
anonymity and obscurity
over a lifetime of hosannas
and obsequious deference,
wanting to be one of us
in a most ordinary way
born homeless and in filth,
dispossessed and marginal.

True Magesterium.

Some Thoughts for
An Institutional Church

Any attempts to channel all of human life,
to regulate the flow of
feelings, seeing, thinking, acting
within compulsive dogmatic routines
will fail.

Hierarchy
will be neither rejected, nor mocked
if it is a hierarchy of Values
not merely proclaimed,
but lived.

Authority will not be denied
insofar as it expresses
Truth and Reality
and manifests
Wisdom and Compassion.

Inter-religious dialogue
will remain fruitless
unless based on
a radically open witness
to any authentic religious experiences.

Institutional Egos
can be discounted and overcome
when value is placed on
Experience and Intuition.

Conflict within the institution
will prevail as long as
Linguistic Chauvinism,
Cerebral Theological Conceits,
and Narcissism
are modes of existence.

Anxieties about
Preservation of Institutional Identity
Highlight the depth of delusion
about group ego.

Pervasive indoctrination
of contempt and animosity
towards the Others
precludes
Spiritual Connection and Growth.

The Western emphasis on Being
and
The Eastern emphasis on non-Being, Void,
are complementary expressions
of Truth and Reality,
and are not mutually exclusive.

Freedom Quest

I seek freedom,
freedom from my views,
even what I believe to be my right views.

For the Right View
Is truly defined as
the absence of all views.

I try not to be attached;
even attached to dogma.

I try to let go;
even let go of knowledge
so as to be open.

For if I believe I have reached truth,
and attach to it,
I will no longer have any chance
to reach Truth.

I may use knowledge
as a raft
to cross the river,
being willing to abandon it
once crossed.

Irony

Just as

Banks make some people
Poor,

Hospitals make some people
Sick,

and

Schools make some people
Ignorant,

So

Church makes some people
Evil.

CHURCH

It is like Noah's ark:

Not where the saved gather,

But where all can come
To be saved.

The stench in the ark (church)
would be unbearable

if it were not for
the storm outside.

Mystery

Religion is in the mystery business.
If there were no mystery in the world,
there would be no need for religion.
One must wonder then why
on both the left and the right,
there is so much effort
to take the mystery out of religion,
to reduce it either to rules
taken out of context from the scripture
or to explanations
which theologians think
will persuade those influenced by science
that religion is not absurd.

Religion is indeed absurd, but only
because our existence is absurd.
How come we're here, anyway?
How come there is anything at all,
anyway?
Religion is a cautious attempt
to respond to mystery
with something better than the suspicion
that it is a tale told by an idiot,
full of sound and fury
and signifying nothing,
if only with the modest,

"there is something afoot in the universe,
something that looks like
gestation and birth."

Religion is the unpretentious affirmation
in the face of
substantial contrary evidence
that God is not mad
and ask why
She seems to know so much higher math.

It is the attempt to face the odd fact
that the evolutionary process
has produced minds
that are capable of comprehending
(if just barely) both General Relativity and
Quantum Theory,
when there was no advantage
in our evolutionary past
of having such an intellect.

Religion is finally a tentative response to
the question, "how come, anyway?"

Many theologians, still a little breathless
and a little late,
think that science is in the process of
eliminating mystery.

When *the answer* is found
we will not be able to understand it.
Nonetheless it is clear that the more we
know about reality
the more mysterious it seems.

Only those who want to use the bible to
explain away mystery
or those who think that's what religion does
(not without some reason)
can imagine there is a conflict
between science and religion
when in fact both of them bump their
heads against the solid wall of mystery
and increasingly both think they hear
murmurs of one kind or another
from beyond that wall.

Religion therefore must be open
(once again?) to mystery.

It is a mistake in our religious services to
eliminate all openness to the marvelous,
the wonderful, the surprising,
to dispense with the poetic,
the imaginative,
the metaphorical dimensions of religion,
to exclude its experiential and

the narrative aspects,
to forget that religion is poetry
and story before it is anything else and
after everything else.

The search for religious experience
and for the meaning
of religious experience
seems to have increased.

Religious experience may have become
disconnected with prosaic religion
and therefore much of the search
is for links between religion and experience
which were once more obvious.

Clergy persons seem to assume
that their congregations are completely
spirit-less
and that it is their function to reshape them
in the clergy person's own image and
likeness
so that they give the same answers to
questions we propose
and which they are unlikely to ever ask
on their own.

In fact religious experience is endemic
in our society,
most of it part of and the result
of ordinary experiences of life
and almost none of it drug-induced.

The Holy is everywhere,
even if people don't know who (or Who)
it is.
Religion arises from experiences of the Holy
and takes its raw power
from such experiences.

Religion is poetry before it is prose
because poetry is inevitable
in telling stories about the experience
of mystery.
Yet religious leaders think that it is their job
to replace poetry with prose,
to clarify the experiential with
the propositional,
and to explain stories immediately and
thus explain them away.
It seems to me that it is the task of clergy
persons to listen to their people
as they tell stories of their experiences
of the Holy,
their explorations into mystery

and then to correlate their stories
with the overarching stories
of the Heritage,
often through community ritual.

The emphasis here is on listening,
on keeping our mouths shut,
and on resisting
the almost incurable temptation
to stretch the stories
on to our theological categories.

Why, I wonder,
are we so afraid of mystery?
Why are we so eager to budget
the Holy Spirit's time for Her
when on the record
She is determined to blow whither she will?

I am not asserting that reason and
reflection should be abandoned.
We are reflecting creatures.
We need doctrines and catechisms and
creeds and theologies
(even, in limited amounts, theologians),
and even some kind of teaching authority.

We must go through our critical period
between the first and the second naiveté.

We must not fixate,
as clergy and theologians
often seem to do,
between the two naivetés.

It may be possible to encounter and
respect mystery
without art and music and story and ritual.

However, too many seem to think
that one can and should,
although our heritage has always believed
the exact opposite,
from the New Testament hymns on.

Gleaned from an article
by and with the approval of
Andrew Greeley

The Answer

Jesus was asked
several hundred questions
in the Gospels.
He directly answered
three.

His life,
His ministry,
His message
was not one of providing people with
answers.

Jesus' idea of Church
is a state of longing and yearning for God
and for us finding Wisdom
in our own souls.

Jesus' answer to the myriad of Questions
is the same:
The Holy Spirit.

What we pray for we might obtain,
but Jesus promises us
that we will receive
The Holy Spirit.

Only God is in control.

New Ways

My heart aches with the state of
Our Church.

The hierarchy would suffocate us with
control.

Rigidity prevents it finding
contemporary solutions to contemporary
challenges.

The institutional dread of deviating from
orthodoxy
inhibits, indeed, prohibits us
from using the Holy Spirit's Gifts
of Imagination and Creativity.

The bureaucratic suppression of Our
Church
will be laid to rest in the pages of history,
a mere chapter
that leads to another unfolding of the
Christian Story.

I'm driven to help hasten its demise
but also prepare for the inevitable:

the Birth of New Ways to be Church.

Openness

Those who adhere
to specific religious doctrines
may feel threatened
by globalization,
by the world becoming localized at an
increasing rate,
by other religious beliefs.

Often, they retreat into fundamentalist
enclaves
denying any possibility of
Enrichment through Diversity.

Some, like St. Basil the Great, believe that
the integrity of religious experience
can be preserved by
an appreciation for different faiths,
reflecting a deep understanding of
one's own faith.

Sipping from even the most exotic flowers
Is not a source of corruption,
but indeed, an opening into

The Life of the Spirit
at the source of
all True Religion.

Path to an Accountable Church

We must first
recognize and name our oppression.
This beginning of the movement
from being victims of history
as defined by someone else
to becoming subject of our own history
is called
Conscientization.

We must reclaim our adulthood
from those who have reinforced
infantilization of the Laity.

We must achieve
A Voice in the Church,
to be taken seriously
on a par with other voices,
clerical, priestly, Episcopal.

We must voice
our vast reservoir of
Practical Wisdom
Theologically and Ethically.

We must
cast aside
attempts by hierarchy to stifle debate.

Let us

take the emphasis off Church as Institution
and

Live it more as Community,
People of God,
Inclusive rather than Exclusive,

locating the Heart of Church

in the Life of the Community,

not in organization.

Priesthood

The degeneration of priestly fraternity

into

self-serving clerical solidarity

and

the prevalence of managerial concerns

over authentic pastoral charity

are

systemic evils.

By Germain Grisez, theologian

Addressed to North American Bishops

Before their meeting in Dallas, 2002.

Priestly Grief

So much of Church teaching
fails to reach people where they are,

Most priests agree with their parishioners.

Priests are called upon to be
A Focus of Unity
in A Church

when deep mutual suspicion
creates extreme polarization.

The Laity
overwhelmingly blame the Bishops
for the sexual abuse crisis

while priests bear the brunt of the penalty
with little or no support
from on high.

Priests' Grief

Our priests
Like us

Grieve

The passages of life,
The loss of youth,
The passing of the middle years,
The loss of health,

They Grieve

The loss of Integrity
occasioned by fear or cowardice

The wife and family
sacrificed to mandatory celibacy

The loss of trust and confidence
following the abuse scandals

The failed leadership of their bishops

The Church's inability to listen
to the anguished voices of women

The loss of morale
occurring with their bishops' unwillingness
to listen to them

Overwork

Being misunderstood

Reality

Dear Bishops,

We are not dissident Catholics.

We are the Core and Foundation,
We are Parish Council members,
We are the Parish Finance Council,
We are the Confirmation and
Religious Ed Teachers,
We are Lectors and Eucharistic Ministers.

We are the Core of the Catholic Church.

We are your greatest Asset
because
We care enough to fight.

Dialogue with us.

No agenda.
No lawyers,
No mandates,
No press.

Dialogue with us newly vitalized Catholics;
We have proven our Love for the Church
and our Parishes.

Listen to us.

Listen without expecting to have
all the answers
to our concerns, dreams, and visions.

Perhaps our Dialogue
will point the way to some

new directions,
new structures,
new transparency,
new accountability.

The old way
resulted in a mess
of
distrust and upheaval.

Religion's Demise

Blame not Science for religion's demise
(More scientists than bishops espouse
the mystical).

Blame not our culture,
nor some anti-religious philosophy,
for the eclipse of religion
in modern society.

It is more Honest
to blame religious leaders for its defeat.

Religion has declined,
not because it has been rejected,
but because
its hierarchy has made it
Irrelevant,
Dull,
Oppressive, and
Insipid.

Bishops have replaced
Faith with Greed,
Worship with Discipline,
Love with Conformity and Exclusiveness.

Crises of the day are ignored
by those in power
in favor of some splendor of the Past.

Faith has been made into an Heirloom,
rather than a Living Fountain,
with religious leaders seeking
Museum-keepers
rather than Gardeners,
tending God's living ever-changing
Garden.

Religious leaders speak only with
a voice of Authority,
rather than the Voice of Compassion,
and thus,
have made religion
meaningless.

Righting the wrongs of centuries.

Official Church is guilty of misogyny,
in its theology,
in its interpretation of scripture,
in its exclusion of women
from any significant position
in Church governance,
even in its history,
which has scanted women's contributions
to the Church in every sphere.

The new pope has a duty
to encourage
the preservation of female memory and
tradition,
and the uprooting of a false tradition
which has made women
the sources of sin and temptation
and the dwelling place of evil.

John Paul II reversed many of the strides
made after Vatican II
toward equality of women in the Church.
A good many women have completed
degrees in pastoral ministry,
but, in the latter years of John Paul's reign,
found themselves shut out of priest-less
parishes that sorely needed them.

Why do we have thousands of
unemployed lay ministers
- most of them women –
unless it is more preferable
to close parishes
than to allow women
to maintain the very lifeblood of
a communal Church?

The new pope
has to address the women's question.
It is a major issue of our time.

Recognizing it can only strengthen this
papacy and this Church.

The papacy, and church-official, can only
be diminished by ignoring it.

Silent Oppression

Catholic Tradition
squanders Lay Experience.

Laypeople
have neither active, nor passive voice.

Laypeople are not elected to office
in the Church,
nor do we vote.

Understandable
when Clergy were educated,
Lay Not.
Hardly so, today.

Why no organized attempt to change this?

The systemic
and structural
oppression of the Laity

The division between clergy and laity
in Catholic Tradition
systematically subordinates and
undervalues Lay
lifestyle, talent, leadership, experience,
and Spirituality.

Though the hierarchy would never admit it
publicly,
their patterns of behavior
and the structures
within the Catholic Church
treat the Laity
as if they have lesser talent and
are of lesser account.

Spirituality/Sexuality

Human Sexuality
once was perceived as
A component of the Spiritual,
A Central aspect of it.

Everything in existence
Springs forth from the Cosmic Womb of
Unlimited Possibility.

The Spiritual and Sexual capacity
of humans
Flows from the Spiritual Energy
Of Creation
Opening Faith.

Sexuality
is about a deep capacity for
Love.

Religions have dishonored
Sexuality, Spirituality, Creativity,
by maintaining that
God has nothing to do with Sexuality.

Religions urge us to
Transcend Eros and passion
rather than to
Integrate them into our Living.

Religious Creeds
demonize
Goddess
A Central Figure of our Ancient Ancestors
because of her
Incredible capacity for
Sexuality and Creativity.

We need to rediscover
what Sexuality is all about.
When we honor
The Sacred Mystery of Sexuality,
We embrace the deepest human mystery
and
God's Divine Mystery.

Sexuality
is about
Creativity.

Spirituality
Honors the Whole Person.

Religion tends to offer
only otherworldly utopias,
ideals of unreachable perfection.

We need
Connection
Here and Now.

The primary sin
is not disobedience,
But
Disconnection.

Surprise

I have been trying
to figure out
by whose authority
the hierarchy in place
sets all these rules

to Exclude people.

Jesus
defied the hierarchy in-place
at his time
with His rampant

Inclusiveness.

Alas,
I have found the culprits;
It is us.

Not only do we empower
the abusers,
we pay for it.

Enough!

The Clergy

More darkness and division
have come into the world
amongst the clergy of the holy church
than from any other cause.

In cases of evildoing,
they pretend not to see.

The root of self-love
is alive in them.

Because they fear to lose their position
or their temporal goods,
or their prelacy,
they . . . act like blind ones,
in that they see not the real,
so that their positions will be kept.

With a perverted hope
in their own small knowledge,
they spend so much time
in acquiring and preserving
temporal things,
that they turn their back on the spiritual.

They fulfill the words:

These are blind
and
leaders of the blind
and if the blind lead the blind,
they both fall into the ditch.

By
St. Catherine of Siena
in 1370.

Truth

St. John of the Cross
says that If I am to find that
which I do not have,
I must take a path I do not know.

If I can put myself aside,
divest myself of
my habits, my knowledge, my memories,
I can be free
to make all things new
or at least,
make a place
where all things might be made new.

If only I can learn
not to seek happiness
beyond the present mystery.

Without my ego,
my identity
will continually inform me.

In the present moment,
I can realize
the unknown universality
of human nature.

But, it is more than just
divesting my consciousness
of judgments, desires, purposes.
It is more than just negating
what I already think I know.

It is a matter of wanting to know what I
don't
in a different purer way.
I need a more direct access
to reality.

The whole Truth will always elude me,
remain unknown.

My poetry allows me to be somewhat
content with
partial truth,
glimpses,
indications,
approximations,
analogies,
metaphors
of Truth.

My search
is one of Feeling,
not as emotion,
but as a faculty of my soul.

My search
Is intuitively conceived,
inward, immediate, blind,
sensation.

It allows me a
Oneness.

It opens me
to Love.

And
it seems that any
Spiritual Growth
occurs only in
the present moment.

On my search,
I must let go.
I must become
empty, receptive, simple, humble.

I have learned that
Faith is not a content of belief,
but simply accepting
my unknowing
of the infinite certitude of
ultimate reality.

My Acts of Faith,
performed without desire,
are my acts of Love.

I used to think of Truth as
disclosure, opening, clearing.
But in every opening to Truth,
Truth simultaneously withdraws.

Every un-concealment of it
contains concealment.

Light needs darkness,
Is a darkness.

Reality escapes my every grasp,
deceiving me,
running through my fingers,
despite my need to hold it
in some way.

I can only engage Truth
by leaving it unknown,
by not taking hold of it.

I must suspend, reject, negate,
and go beyond
every answer.

There is no end
to this journey of unknowing,
of non-knowledge.

For whatever I seek,
I must also seek its opposite.

As Mary,
I must wait in unknowing.
I must assent to
humility, poverty of spirit,
nothingness,
through
patience, simplicity, trust
and offer my will
to the Divine Will.

To find the Truth,
perpetually hidden,
I must myself hide,
I must become mystery.

Vatican Contradictions
(Inspired by and gleaned from writings of
Hans Kung)

The festive mood that prevailed
during the Second Vatican Council
(1962 to 1965),
has disappeared.

Vatican II's outlook of renewal,
ecumenical understanding and
a general opening of the world
now seems overcast and
the future gloomy.

Many have resigned themselves
or even turned away out of frustration
from this self-absorbed hierarchy.

As a result, many people are confronted
with an impossible set of alternatives:
"play the game or leave the church."

New hope will only begin to take root
when church officials in Rome
reorient themselves
toward the compass of the Gospel.

HUMAN RIGHTS

Outwardly, the Vatican supports
human rights,
while inwardly withholding them from
bishops, theologians and
especially women.

The Vatican -- once a resolute foe of
human rights,
but nowadays all too willing
to become involved in European politics –
has yet to sign the European Council's
Declaration of Human Rights.
Far too many canons of
the absolutist Roman church law of
the Middle Ages
would have to be amended first.
The concept of separation of powers,
the bedrock of all modern legal practice,
is unknown in the Roman Catholic church.

Due process is an unknown entity
in the church.
In disputes,
one and the same Vatican agency
functions as
lawmaker, prosecutor and judge.

Consequences:
Church suffers with a servile episcopate
and intolerable legal conditions.
Any pastor, theologian or layperson who
enters into a legal dispute with the higher
church courts
has virtually no prospects of prevailing.

THE ROLE OF WOMEN
The Vatican preaches a noble concept of
womanhood,
but at the same time forbids women from
practicing birth control and
bars them from ordination.

Consequences:

There is a rift between external conformism
and internal autonomy of conscience.
This results in bishops
who lean towards Rome,
alienating themselves from women,
as was the case in the dispute surrounding
the issue of abortion counseling
This in turn leads to a growing exodus
among those women
who have so far
remained faithful to the church.

SEXUAL MORALS

The Vatican, while preaching against
mass poverty and suffering in the world,
makes itself partially responsible
for this suffering
as a result of attitudes
toward birth control and
explosive population growth.
The Vatican has declared opposition to
the pill and condoms.

As a result,
It can be held partly responsible for
uncontrolled population growth
and the spread of AIDS in Africa.

Consequences:
Even in traditionally Catholic countries like
Ireland, Spain and Portugal,
the Roman Catholic church's rigorous
sexual morals are openly or tacitly
rejected.

CELIBACY AMONG PRIESTS
By propagating the traditional image of
the celibate male priest,
The Vatican itself bears responsibility for the
catastrophic dearth of priests,
the collapse of spiritual welfare
in many countries,
and the many pedophilia scandals
the church is no longer able to cover up.

Marriage is still forbidden to men
who have agreed to devote their lives
to the priesthood.

This is only one example of how the
Vatican ignores teachings of the bible and
the great Catholic tradition of
the first millennium,
which did not require office bearers to
take a vow of celibacy.
If someone, by virtue of his office, is forced
to spend his life without
a wife and children,
there is a great risk that
healthy integration of sexuality will fail,
which can lead to pedophilic acts.

Consequences:
The ranks have been thinned and there is a
lack of new blood in the Catholic Church.
Soon almost two-thirds of parishes,
will be without an ordained pastor and
regular celebrations of the Eucharist.
It's a deficiency
that even the declining influx of priests
from other countries

and the combining of parishes into
"spiritual welfare units,"

a highly unpopular trend
among the faithful,
can no longer hide.
The average age of active priests today is
now above 60.

ECUMENICAL MOVEMENT
The Vatican outwardly supports
the ecumenical movement.
At the same time, however,
It weighs heavily on relations with orthodox
and reform churches,
and refuses to recognize
their ecclesiastical offices and
Communion services.

The Vatican could have heeded
the advice of several ecumenical
study commissions
and follow the practice of
many local pastors

by recognizing the offices and
Communion services of
non-Catholic churches
and permitting Eucharistic hospitality and
the Inclusiveness of Jesus.

It could have toned down the excessive,
medieval claim to power,
in terms of doctrine and church leadership,
vis-à-vis eastern European churches and
reform churches.
Instead, the Vatican preserves and even
expands the Roman power system.
For this reason,
Rome's politics of power and prestige
are veiled by
ecumenical
soapbox speeches and empty gestures.

Consequences:
Ecumenical understanding was blocked
after the council,
and relations with the Orthodox and
Protestant churches
were burdened to an appalling extent.

The papacy, like its predecessors in the
11th and 16th centuries,
proved to be the greatest obstacle to unity
among Christian churches
in freedom and diversity.

PERSONNEL
The Vatican has disregarded
the collegiality
which had been agreed
and instead celebrates the triumph of
the papacy at the cost of the bishops.

Instead of using
the conciliatory program words
"Aggiornamento –
Dialogue and Collegiality -- ecumenical,"
what's valid now in doctrine and practice
is
"restoration,
lectureship,
obedience and
re-Romanization."

The criteria for the appointment of a
bishop
is not the spirit of the gospel or
pastoral open-mindedness,
but rather to be absolutely loyal to
the party line in Rome.
Before their appointment.
their fundamental conformity is tested
based on a curial catalog of questions
and they are sealed
through a personal and unlimited pledge
of obedience to the Pope
that is tantamount to
an oath to the "Fuehrer."

Consequences:

A largely mediocre, ultra-conservative and
servile episcopate
is possibly the most serious burden of this
overly long pontificate.
The masses of cheering Catholics
at the best-staged Pope manifestations
should not deceive:

Millions have left the church
or they have withdrawn from religious life
in opposition.

CLERICALISM

In the papal campaign of evangelization,
which centers on a sexual morality that is
out of step with the times.

Women, in particular,
who do not share the Vatican's position on
controversial issues
like birth control, abortion, divorce and
artificial insemination
are disparaged as promoters of
a "culture of death."
As a result of its interventions –
the Roman Curia created the impression
that it has little respect for
the legal separation of church and state.

Instead of entering the social mainstream
everywhere by supporting
reasonable solutions,
the Roman Curia, through its
proclamations and secret agitation
is in fact fueling the polarization
between the pro-life and
pro-choice movements,
between moralists and libertines.

Consequences:
Rome's clericalist policy merely strengthens
the position of dogmatic anti-clericalists
and fundamentalist atheists.
It also creates suspicion among believers
that religion could be being misused
for political ends.

NEW BLOOD IN THE CHURCH
the Vatican has drawn in large part on
the conservative "new movements"
of Italian origin,
the "Opus Dei" movement
that originated in Spain,
and an uncritical public loyal to the pope.

The major regional and international youth
events sponsored by
the new lay movements
(Focolare, Comunione e Liberazione, St.
Egidio, Regnum Christi)
and supervised by the church hierarchy
attracted hundreds of thousands
of young people,
many of them well-meaning
but far too many uncritical.
In times when they lack convincing
leadership figures,
these young people are most impressed by
a shared "event."
The personal magnetism of A Pope
is usually more important than
the content of the pope's speeches,
while their effects on parish life are
minimal.

In keeping with the ideal of a uniform and
obedient church,
the Vatican sees the future of the church
almost exclusively
in these easily controlled, conservative
lay movements.

This includes the Vatican's distancing itself
from the Jesuit order,
which is oriented toward
the tenets of the council.
Preferred by earlier popes, the Jesuits,
because of their intellectual qualities,
critical theology and
liberal theological options.
The Jesuits are now perceived as spoilers in
the works of the papal restoration policy.
Instead the Vatican places full confidence
in the financially powerful and influential,
but undemocratic and secretive
Opus Dei movement,
a group linked to fascist regimes in the past
and now especially active in
the world of finance, politics and
journalism.
In fact, by granting Opus Dei
special legal status,
the Vatican even made the organization
exempt from supervision
by the church's bishops.

Consequences:

Young people from church groups and congregations

(with the exception of alter servers),

and especially the non-organized "average Catholics,"

usually stay away from major youth get-togethers.

Catholic youth organizations

at odds with the Vatican

are disciplined and starved

when local bishops, at Rome's behest, withhold their funding.

The growing role of the archconservative and non-transparent

Opus Dei movement

in many institutions

has created a climate of uncertainty and suspicion.

Once-critical bishops have cozied up to Opus Dei,

while laypeople

who were once involved in the church have withdrawn in resignation.

SINS OF THE PAST

The baroque and bombastic confession of
the church's transgressions,
staged with cardinals in
St. Peter's Cathedral,
remained vague, non-specific and
ambiguous.

The pope only asked for forgiveness for
the transgressions of the
"sons and daughters" of the church,
but not for those of the "Holy Fathers,
" those of the "church itself"
and those of the
hierarchies present at the event.

The Vatican has never commented on the
Curia's dealings with the Mafia,
and in fact contributed more to covering
up than uncovering scandals and
criminal behavior.
The Vatican has also been extremely slow
to prosecute pedophilia scandals involving
Catholic clergy.

Consequences:
The half-hearted confession remained
without consequences,
producing neither reversals nor action,
only words.

The Vatican's contradictions,
have deeply polarized the church,
alienating it from countless people and
plunged it into an epochal crisis
a structural crisis that,
after a quarter century,
is now revealing fatal deficits
in terms of development and
a tremendous need for reform.

Contrary to all intentions conveyed in the
Second Vatican Council,
the medieval Roman system,
a power apparatus with
totalitarian features,
was restored
through clever and ruthless personnel and
academic policies.

Bishops were brought into line,
pastors overloaded,
theologians muzzled,
the laity deprived of their rights,
women discriminated against,
national synods and churchgoers' requests
ignored,
along with sex scandals,
prohibitions on discussion,
liturgical spoon-feeding,
a ban on sermons by lay theologians,
incitement to denunciation,
prevention of Holy Communion.

The upshot is that
the Catholic church has completely lost
the enormous credibility
it once enjoyed
under the papacy of John XXIII
and in the wake of
the Second Vatican Council.

If the new pope were to continue the
policies of the last pontificate,
he would only reinforce an enormous
backup of problems
and turn the Catholic church's
current structural crisis into
a hopeless situation.

Instead, the new pope must decide
in favor of a change in course
and inspire the church
to embark on new paths
-- in the spirit of John XXIII
and in keeping with the impetus for reform
brought about by
the Second Vatican Council.

Museum or Garden

John XXIII urged us all
not to be museum keepers,
not to try to protect
that which was,
not to spend our lives
dusting off relics
of times gone by
at the expense of what is to be.

John XXIII instead urged us all
to be God's gardeners,
to tend the ever-growing
and hence ever-changing
garden of life
that is Creation,
that is Church.

John XXIII
tried to help make church
all that it can be,
while others, even now,
seem more intent
on trying to make Church
what it was

John XXIII, the penultimate Pro-Lifer.

Un-proclaimed Heroines

(Women in Scriptures about whom
we rarely hear on Sundays in Church)

Shiprah and Puah were
Midwives who bravely resisted the
Pharaoh's
order to kill all male Hebrew children.
Where would Moses be,
Where would we be
if these women were submissive?
(Exodus)

Who was Huldah?
Only a Prophet!
(Kings)

The Mother of the Maccabee brothers had
Valor "most admirable and worthy of
Everlasting Remembrance."
(Maccabees)

Esther and Judith
were not just stereotypic females,
but, indeed, Heroes.
Esther's Bravery saved her people.

Judith had not only beauty and
asceticism,
but also Initiative, Determination, and
Courage.

The Woman anointing Jesus' head
(Matthew)
is to be "spoken of in memory of her
wherever the good news is proclaimed
throughout
the world" said Jesus.
"Go to my brothers and tell them."
said by Jesus to Mary of Magdala
is not heard on Easter Sunday.
This important Apostolic Commission
Is unheard on Easter.

Jesus was "abandoned by everyone"
we hear.
Everyone except by women
who were invisible and discounted
even today in our Church.

We belong to the Church beneath the church.

Ratzinger has said many things
he will now have to iron out as

"pope of all the people"

such as his saying in a Paris interview that
'Buddhism is a form of auto-eroticism,"

"homosexuals only deserve limited rights,"

"homosexuality is a 'tendency' toward an
'intrinsic moral evil."

He muzzled liberation theologians in
central and south America,

causing suffering and death there.

According to him, "Hinduism offers

'false hope."

He has said that other Christian religions
are not true religion.

We follow the Christ. Not Paul. Not Peter.
Not men. Not Popes.

We follow the Christ.

That's why we are called Christians,

and not Pedros, Paolists, Hombrists or
Papists.

In this time too, let us follow our Christ and
think and act as much as we can, like Him.

Acting like Him:

being mocked and harmed,

to healing the sick,

to teaching and loving,

to roaring back to life.

We have been in agony for many years

and we have practically perfected the
knack of resurrection,

in the name of Our Lord, who taught us.

Lost Mission

It seems that any organization,

commercial, governmental, private,
or religious

over a period of time

ends up with its prime objective being

Perpetuating the Organization
(usually as it is)

and

Protecting the Jobs of those running it

completely losing site

of the original Mission
for which the organization was created.

Look at
Our Government,
Our Corporations,
Our Church.

We Want it Back!

Jesus Christ started it all
by calling us to priesthood.

We lived our faith
and worshipped together
sometimes in hiding,
often in our homes.

We celebrated Eucharist together
in many ways
in many places.

Somewhere along the way
We abandoned church
to a group of celibate male clerics,
to a hierarchy of power.

As is typical with hierarchical organizations,
the mission was lost
for the sake of perpetuating the
organization
and the jobs within.

We ended up worshipping
only where and how the hierarchy told us
we could,
or for most,
not at all.

The people to whom we entrusted church
have screwed it up.

And now we want it back!

The Holy Spirit
--clearly on our side—
is helping us retrieve our church
by helping us take it over at the grass roots
and
by concluding the all-male all-celibate
ordained priesthood.

We want our Church back
And
We'll get it!

Whither Lay Ministry?

I Retired after thirty-two years as
a successful Corporate Executive
having Lived and Traveled abroad
extensively.

Relatively Young,
Healthy,
Financially Secure,
I felt called to devote my gifts
and balance of my time
to Others.

I Volunteered with Hospice
and began a New Life
helping Any in Grief
and
those wishing to be better
Caregivers.

Lay Ministry?

I Explored Deaconate,
finding roadblock after roadblock after
roadblock:
no national program (lived six months each
in two states),

mixed use of Deacons by Bishops,
many frustrated Deacons,
yes-men only want yes-men under them,
simon-pure background required.

Many told me
I would be many times more effective
unbound from ties of ordination.

Pastoral Minister to the Bereaved?
No such ministry recognized.

In the meantime,
calls for my Counseling, Support Groups,
Workshops, In-Service, Training, Retreats,
and Talks
grew every year.

Earned a Certificate in Spirituality
from a Diocesan Institute,
earned a Masters Degree
in Pastoral Ministries
from a Catholic University
(completing a totally Catholic
formal education
Grammar, High, College, and Post Grad)

All on my own financially
with all of my Workshops, etc offered for
free-will honorariums only.

Published five books
on my own spiritual journey
(This is number six)

Added numerous workshops
on Spirituality and Spiritual Growth
in response to lack of such
being addressed by Institutional Church.

Lay Ministry?
Bishops decided to recognize only
Lay Ecclesial Ministers
which I was not.

Nonetheless,
my ministry grew and grew and grew,
being asked to speak and facilitate
all across the country.

Actually invited to Preach
at a number of protestant churches,
though not allowed by my own.

Led Communion Services
even though Bishop frowned upon them
as blurring the distinction
twixt ordained and not.

Conducted successful retreats
on Grief and on Spirituality.

Lay Minister?

Only in the freelance sense.

Most assuredly with the Guidance
and Prodding
of the Holy Spirit
but
unrecognized and unsupported
and sometimes
even rejected
by Church Official.

And so we work from outer edge
of the Circle of Church Official
Sometimes from within
Sometimes from outside

Always
with a Focus to Ministering to Others
regardless of
the rules, the boundaries, the exclusions,
the sanctions, the formulas.

Individual pastors of many churches
Welcome my help.

Lay Minister?

I'm not ordained—or even recognized
by Church Official,
but
I am Lay
and
I do try my best to Minister to Others
and so I continue on

trying to keep the Tree that is Church
healthy at its grass roots
regardless of which red bird
Is perched atop.

I just wonder how many others
could similarly help
with even a little encouragement or
support by
Church Official.

Ministry

We soon will be getting
Yet another paper by the Bishops
on Lay Ministry

How about a paper by the Laity
on the Church Hierarchical Ministry?

How does a supposedly Loving
Clerical Ministry
allow the Bishops
to permit the molestation of youths
by priests to go on
without notification
of law enforcement officials
or notification to the Catholic Community
at large?

How does a supposedly transparent
Clerical Ministry
come to believe that Bishops
could transfer abusing priests,
hide the records of abuse,
and remain credible leaders
of anything?

How does a supposedly compassionate
Clerical Ministry
allow Bishops
to re-victimize the abused
with cruel counter suits?

How does a supposedly accountable
Clerical Ministry
allow Bishops
to secretly raid the community's treasury
to buy silence?

How does a supposedly responsible
Clerical Ministry
allow these Bishops
to go on acting as leaders
without a full and personal accounting
to the Community
they are supposed to Serve?

Methinks we need a paper
on
Arrogant Clericalism.

Spirituality

A great discovery for me is that
a fundamental requirement
of True Spirituality
is
Engagement with the World
whether it be
Family, Village, Nation, or Planet.

Such involvement
marks authentic Spirituality
and helps cultivate and spread it.

A Spirituality
that does not dirty its hands
with the muck of daily human life,
is not human.

To my amazement,
True Spirituality
is inherently communal,
in constant need of testing
against the practices and beliefs
of others.

An authentic Spirituality
is as inter-dependent on others
as is our inter-dependence on others
for food and other necessities of life.

Church exists
not for its members,
but for the Whole Human Family.

I am learning to resist the temptation
to see Church as some sort of safe haven
guaranteeing goodies for her members.

Christian Spirituality will only flourish
when we look outward
and share the joy, grief, and anguish
of all people.

Change

The notion that

Humanity is in a state of "becoming,"
That
We are "in process,"
poses a threat
To those who are in power,
Those who wish to cling to power.

Christianity is a "Movement,"
A "Transformation."

So, the Eucharist
must be constantly reinvigorated
to be relevant to people in their own
cultures;

Unjust social attitudes and structures
must be challenged if they diminish
people;

Patterns of domination and oppression,
outside and within the Church,

must be opposed.

Crisis

The crisis
of institutional Church
is the autistic notion that

The Sacramental World
is contained and controlled solely within
the members of the hierarchy;

that they are the chosen ones,
called from eternity
to save Church by supervising it.

The institutional hierarchy
are so focused on their own centrality,
that they distort
Sacraments.

Instead of richly human Sacramentality,
sensual, sexual and spiritual,

They abuse the Body of Christ
by closing and merging our churches and
by deforming personality into
antagonistic elements of spirit and flesh,
attempting to foist on us
"antidotes" for being human,

rather than
Sacraments which nourish and nurture
our full humanity.

We are being offered
not the ecstasy and passion of
Teresa of Avila or
John of the Cross,

not the Excitement of Transformation,

but instead
ceremonies
paved with the literal
rather than the sacramental,
laced with chords of law and precedent
rather than the lyrical,
void of mystery borne by story or symbol.

A renewal of the Sacramental Life
of institutional Church

requires

a Truthful, Open, Collegial Relationship
with
God's People.

Freedom

The higher up you are in the system
the more trapped you are.

The more you're outside the system.
the Freer you are.

For every promotion or recognition
you accept,
there is a price: more party line.

That is true for business and
almost any organization,
including the Church.

A bishop never gets two things:
a bad meal or the Truth.

When you're high up in anything,
you are expected to represent it,
hold it together,
affirm it.

You would likely be irresponsible
if you didn't.

So, the Spiritual Greats, like Jesus, just say,
"Avoid it!"

The price of Truth can be very great.

But we say what is needed to survive and
to be liked inside the group and
to hold the group in unity,.

Blessed are the Poor in Spirit,
who don't have to play these games.

The Kingdom of Heaven isn't later,
It's now
for those who remain
without anything to protect or
anything you need to prove or
to defend.

Richard Rohr
On the Beatitudes of the Poor in Spirit
From "Jesus Plan for a New World."

Why Me?

All I wanted to do was
Nurture my Spirituality,
to grow spiritually.

In the process,
I gained many insights
important for me
and
I was able to help many others
along the way.

It's the Great Paradox:
In Helping Others
and
I Learned more about
Who I Really Am.

I never intended
to devote one ounce of effort
to trying to change
Institutional Church.

I'd leave that to others,
all I wanted to do
was help others
wherever I could.

Let the ecclesial politicians
worry about the organization,
I thought.

The institution had been good for me
as a child,
as a "Conventional-Wisdom" Catholic.
For most of my life,
Pray, Pay and Obey (most of the time)
sufficed.

Concurrent with my Spiritual Growth
(chronicled elsewhere)
and perhaps related to it
(I'm not sure),
I began to see
the failings, abuses, myopia,
of the institution.

I discovered that
many of the people,
I wanted to try and help,
had been
hurt, abused, alienated, denigrated,
by Institutional Church.

Many wonderful gifts
were left unused;

Many Lights
were being stifled
under bushel baskets.

What could I do
to have one iota of impact
on this mammoth institution?
I really did not want
to get involved,
I just wanted to do what I could
to keep the tree healthy
at the grass roots,
regardless which bird
was perched atop it.

I continued trying to help people
tip their bushel baskets
so their lights could be seen
and shared by the whole world.

Sometimes,
it was institutional church
keeping the lights stifled.

As I grew
I learned
that my memorized Conventional Wisdom
does not work,
that Jesus' Great Gift to us
was not bondage to an Institution,
but Freedom,
Freedom to Love,
Freedom to find our way
up the Mountain of Life.

I learned that each path up the mountain
is unique
and that neither I, nor any one else,
can tell someone how to make their way
up
through the cloud of the unknowing.

Jesus delivered the message of
Love, Freedom, Forgiveness
in an Inclusive, Non-bureaucratic,
Disruptive way,
and Institutional Church
seems to have strayed from
the Essential Mission and
was clearly not Inclusive,
ultra-bureaucratic, and
strove for the Status Quo.

So I've been continuing to
try and tip bushels,
and speak out best I can
against
institutional abuse, domination, and
myopia.

It seems true
that if I don't speak and write
My Truth,
I chip away at my own Integrity.

My efforts may have little impact
on felling Goliath,
but then
I've learned that
The Holy Spirit calls us
out of our comfort zone.

I guess I must be willing to pay the price.
One cleric already cancelled
some of my Grief Support Workshops
in "his" parish
because I dared dissent.
His Loss!

I don't know why me,
but that's ok,
God's in control.

My Church, My Paradox

Is She holy, so full of sinners?

Is She to tear us away from earthly matters
and
remind us
of our eternal vocation
when she is constantly occupied
with things of the earth
as if She wished to live here forever?

Is She truly universal and open in Divine
Intelligence and Charity
when She fosters huddling
in a closed circle?

Does her protection of stability need to
resist and/or ignore
real change in the world?

How can She encourage us
to reach out of ourselves to others
when She seems to inward focused?

Do I let Her pull me in or

Do I strive to pull her out?

A Truly Catholic Church

Christlike
Authentic
Trusting
Heart-dominated
Open
Loving
Inclusive
Compassionate

Changing
Honest
Un-bureaucratic
Realistic
Clear
Hopeful

Peace and Comfort

Jesus Christ did not bring peace and
comfort
to his followers.

He changed the Apostles careers and
lifestyles.

His parables stood them on their heads.

He challenged them
out of their comfort zones.

He chastised their pettiness.
He bemoaned their lack of faith.
He wept at their laziness.
He rebuked their materialness.
He reproached their stinginess
He required more prayer of them.
He reproved their misunderstandings.
He taught them anew.
He grieved their lack of courage.
He worked miracles to convince them.
He suffered at the hands of their betrayal.
He foretold their abandonment of Him.
He dramatically altered their lives forever.

So why do <u>WE</u> expect to leave the Church

comfortable and unchallenged?

Role of the Laity

The role of the laity?
Simple:
To fully serve the needs of each other
using our God-given skills, talents, gifts.

What did we do before we organized
a full-time professional clergy
to do it for us?
We did it all ourselves.

Let's look to the original lay team of
Jesus Christ and the apostles and disciples.
They served the needs of those around
them
with Love and Compassion.
Christ's Servant Leadership was
non-bureaucratic, disruptive, and
inclusive.
Jesus walked his talk:
He showed the role of the laity
by his life.
It was full of Love and Compassion
manifested in Forgiveness.
Could it be any clearer?
Could it be any simpler?
(Simple, perhaps, but not easy.)

What is there in Community (Parishes)
that we laity cannot do for each other?
Across the world,
Lay people are
ministering to the physical, emotional, and
spiritual needy,
teaching, preaching, administrating,
forgiving and blessing one another.
The gifts are given: they need to be
brought from under the bushel basket.

For too long we have abandoned our
responsibilities
to the clergy;
the Holy Spirit is awakening the need for us
to
re-assume them,
once again, to be servant leaders.

Need we let the shrinking cadre of
professional clergy
keep the Sacraments or the sacraments
from people?
The role of the laity?

WWJD?

Jesus was a lay person.

Role of the Pastor

A channel through which the Holy Spirit
Brings Truth to the world
is the Pastor,
who helps teach it to the Laity,
who, in turn translate it and put it
to work in the world.

The problem in the modern church
is that the channel is blocked.

The Pastor does not engage
In the secular world
on a day in, day out basis
and the Lay People
tend to keep their Faith in a compartment
separate from the rest of their lives.

Sunday after Sunday,
congregations sit passively like spectators
watching the entertainment up front,
missing the fact that
they should be absorbing the Truth
and
applying it to their Lives.

St. Paul says
The Pastor is not paid
to do our work (service) for us.

Pastors and Teachers
are to equip the saints (us)
to serve,
to build the Body of the Church,
to Be the Church in the world.

Every Lay person is to be equipped
as a Minister of the Gospel.

Future Church

Parishes will be lay oriented with
shared and collaborative ministry.

Church will not be grounded in
ordination and office,
but more in Baptism and Charism,
binding us disciples in a common mission
with leadership conferred
with broader input
respectful of others' gifts.

Church will be defined relationally,
not numerically or institutionally,
with a personal approach
moving away from divisive extremes
towards the more urgent goal of finding
God.

Church will not be a pyramid;
It will be male/female balanced
with some priests married,
united to people all across the world.

Church will retrieve the Mystical,
stress the Wisdom Tradition and
return to a Holistic Spirituality.

Church will be Spiritually oriented and
less program driven,
with the gifts of Spiritual Direction
more widely scattered.

Church will retrieve a Catholic Imagination
in architecture, liturgy, art, theatre, and
music.

A new Priesthood will arise,
within and among the people,
a common communion in the ministry.

Parishes will downsize,
speak from weakness,
align with the poor,
and foster humility.

Church Education will be
Intergenerational,
not just for children.

Church will be based in Collegiality.

Church will be a male-female relationship.

Future Church!

Sacraments

Sacraments are Celebrations,
Celebrations of something that
has already happened.

A Church does not dispense Grace.

Parents dedicate their child to God
well before the Celebration.
Adult conversion is not dependent
on an immersion.

Young Adults commit to their Faith
well before the laying of hands.

God's Forgiveness is available
before we confess to a priest,
well before we even sin.

God is within us
before reception of the Bread and Wine.

A man and woman
commit Marriage to each other
well before the church celebration.

A person dedicates his/her life to
priesthood
before any Official Appointment.

An ill person can receive the gift of
comfort/healing
before an ordained anointing.
This takes nothing away from the
Celebrations,

They are Beautiful and Powerful and

Vital for the whole Community.

But they are Celebrations of
something that has already happened.

A Church does not dispense Grace.

God does.

Anytime, anywhere, any way
the Holy Spirit chooses.

Church

A role of Church
is to show us
that what we do in our everyday lives
is
Sacred and Holy.

Church should Bless our Lives
and
help us recognize the Holy
in us.

The Holy Spirit
blows where it wants to,
not only in church buildings.

My Family
gathered in Love over the kitchen table
with coffee and cookies
is Eucharistic.

My Friends
gathered in Celebration
with beer and pretzels
is Eucharistic.

My Children and I
making up after a dispute
is Reconciliation.

My Praying and Sharing
with a terminally ill patient
is Sacramental.

My Son and Daughter-in-law
committing themselves to each other in
Love
is Matrimony.

Spiritual Guidance or Leadership
provided by
Marrieds and/or Females
Is Priestly.

Church is

The People of God

wherever we are.

Pentecost

Pentecost completes the mission of Jesus.
Our salvation is achieved
within a human earthly setting
by a Divine Agent, Jesus Christ,
working through
the Power of the Holy Spirit.

Wind, water, fire are striking symbols of
God's Holy Spirit.

Pentecost is a feast of Liberation and
Freedom,
sometimes achieved with pain and
in suffering.
Sometimes, the Spirit's presence is
recognized
only in life's breaking points,
the moments when
our lives seem to come unglued.

Pentecost is feast of unity,
a celebration of peace
in the midst of our ever-present
anxieties, antipathies, and tensions.

The Gift of the Holy Spirit:
Is given to ALL people,

("They were all filled with the Holy Spirit.")
not just Bishops and Priests
not just those of one religion.

Is a gift of Unity,
("They were all with one accord
in one place.")
The Spirit makes the many to be One
in the Body of Christ.
The Holy Spirit reverses
the human condition
started at the tower of Babel.
Individuals are transformed into
Persons capable of relating
to one another.
The Spirit brings Unity and
mutual comprehension.
("They were one in mind and heart.")

Is a gift of Diversity,
given to each directly.
The Spirit makes us, not only One,
but also different.
At Pentecost, various languages
were not abolished,
but they ceased to be a cause of division.

We are called
to realize the distinctive characteristics
of our individual personality
Each of us is called
to be Unique.

Climbing

Climbing the Mountain of Life,
we can use doctrines, dogmas, and
creeds,
to help pull us up over difficult obstacles,
as long as we then untie ourselves
from them

to keep growing.

We don't need permanent hitching posts,
which keep us from reaching our peak.

Tradition offers us
a good footing
from which to move on.

If we simply look around
for others to help up,
Love and Compassion
will push us and pull us

Upward.

Teacher

The Teacher of Spirituality
is Life.

Before it's too late,
see God's Revelation
in our midst.

The world is not an expendable backdrop
to some remote salvation drama.
God is
Here and Now!

Every bush is burning.

God has been at work in Creation
for billions of years
and is still at it.

Religious Fundamentalism
plagues the world
treating the planet and humans
as secondary.
It is not mere scenery to be struck
when the drama is played out.

Creation is the means by which God
communicates with us.

Through created things,
God assails, penetrates, molds us.

Find God in the thousands of things of
creation.

The real miracle is
Our Life.

Be Spiritual

Render others Spiritual

Treat every moment in life with
divine respect

Love passionately

Be astonished
at your brief breathtaking consciousness
of the universe

Thank God every moment
for the tremendous gift of life

Lift your heart to the heavens constantly

Contemplate with wonder the marvelous
creation
all around

Fill your mind, body, soul
with divine trepidation

Know that you are coming from
somewhere
and
that you are going somewhere
in the universal stream of time
Be open and aware

Quest your true self

Treat every living being with divine respect

Pray, Meditate

Be convinced of your death and your
resurrection

Be convinced of Eternal Life

Christist in All

As we learn to discover God
in the center of our being and in all being,
we will find our true relation with all people.

In our center, we find Christ,
who reconciles all people in unity with
Himself.

Christ died for All;
He redeemed All;
He unites All in Him.

Our Faith teaches us
to find His presence in All people.

Our task is to cooperate with
the mystery of grace
seeking to discover the presence of Christ
in every religion, in every soul.

Despite what is said by the hierarchy,
we have more to learn than to teach.

Magisterium can only flow from
Ministerium.

Universality

Christianity
will never realize its full stature
as a genuine Catholicism,
as a universal religion of mankind,
until it has incorporated into itself
all that is true
in all the different religious traditions.

I am learning a deep respect for the truth
which is to be found in all forms of religion.

I am ready to learn from all religions
so that I might understand the significance
of my own.

I do not believe that my religion
is to be restricted to any of
the present forms or expression.

Every religion embodies some aspect of
truth.
Each has something to bring
to the Church.
Though the Church possesses truth,
She is not perfect,
She is not complete.

The Church must extend to all people;
It cannot be named Catholic
if it does not accept as true
every form of piety,
every form of holiness.

There is no person,
from the beginning to the end of the world,
who does not receive Grace from God,
who is not called to Eternal Life with God.
All follow the Light given them.

All religious traditions contain
some elements of Truth.

Where is God

I searched for God
in my complicated, confused,
sometimes chaotic life.

Sure, I found God
in Church, in Sacrament, and
in many Sacred Places and Events.

But I also discovered God
in the ordinary experiences of my life,
where Faith and Life seem to merge.

I found out that
all ground is Holy Ground.

For too much of my life,
I failed to see the preciousness of
each ordinary human experience.

I swam through life,
not fully sensing that
God is near me, with me, in me,
and beyond me.

I could not exist
without God's sustaining Love.

God is a heartbeat away.

God's in the kitchen as well as the chapel,

if I have eyes to see.

Trinity and Us

Since God as Trinity
is a Relational Communitarian Being
We, who are created in
The Image of God
are also at our core

Relational Beings.

God is
Giver, Given, and Gifting
and
Lover, Beloved, Loving
so our life,
if authentically human,
should be the same.

We are who we are,
We become what we are called to
become

in and through

Our Relationship with Others.

Just as the Three Persons of God
are in Communion with each other,
We are called to be
In Communion with Each Other.

How?

When we move toward the world as it is,
When we respond to the needs of others
as it is,
We act as Sons and Daughters of God
In Communion.

We need to foster relationships
that are Equal, Mutual, and
Interdependent
as is Trinity.

A Cross to Bear

Carrying my cross
does not mean
humbly resigning myself to
pain, misery, and sorrow.

It does not mean
accepting life's trials and tribulations,
its challenges and its setbacks
as givens.

It does not mean
wearing my sorrow, sickness, sadness
in order to elicit
sympathy, commiseration and pity.

To me,
Carrying my cross means
expressing the fullness of my faith
despite the chides, mocking, derision,
scorn, jeering
ridiculing, sneering, belittling, and
abuse of others.

To me, it means
being proud enough
to stand up for my faith,
being enthusiastic enough to share it,
being confident enough to express it.

To me, Carrying my Cross means
not accepting the bad things
that happen,
but rising above them and
seeing the good that flows from them
(thanks to God)

I hold up the Cross,
not as a symbol of suffering and death,
but a symbol of resurrected and living
Faith,
a symbol of Joy.

Religion

An immediacy between God and me
is more important for me now
than ever before.

All the societal supports for religion
are collapsing and dying out
in our pluralistic and secular society.

If I am to grow my Christian Spirituality,
it will not be kept alive and healthy
by external helps
(even those offered by church)
but only through my ultimate and
immediate
encounter with God.

Climb Down

I know He is around.
I can feel His presence.
Others must also;
Crowds are gathering.

No way I can approach Him;
My life has been a litany of
faults, failures, sins.
Maybe just a look, a glance.

I need to see Him.
I must.

I think I can climb the tree
and rise above the tumult.

It's a struggle to get high enough,
but if I do I may be able to see Him.

Ah,
It's more peaceful up here, Quieter.
There's less of a hassle here above the
crowd.

There!
I see Him!
I can see Him!

He sees me too.
He looks at me and says,
"John, come down from on high,"
"Descend, for this day I am with you in your house."

Wow!
I thought I had to rise above the others to see Him

and He tells me

To Descend.

He tells me to be with Him

In my own house.

I come down quickly
to my own place
where, indeed,
He is with me.

Aspects, Essence, Distinctions of My Faith

I believe that
God Sanctifies All Aspects of
Our Existence on Earth.

Salvation is not to be found or
holiness not achieved
by scorning reality
or trying to escape all that is human,
but by
Living Life Fully.

By embracing all that is human
(the good and the bad)
all things are transformed by Grace
and
become a means to Redemption.

On the path of Spiritual Growth
we must often descend
in order to ascend.

Often, the way up is down.
The Path is a daily struggle,
a long road
of engaging the world
with ups and downs,
fits and starts.

I believe that God,
Is not only transcendent,
but also
Immanent in the world.

All things that exist,
do so because God created them,
God loves them,
and God sustains them,
and thus
all things have the ability to
communicate the Power and Goodness of
God.

God is intimately with us
in the Eucharist,
and in all circumstances,
and at all times.

The Sacred is Continuous with the secular.

All created things emanate from God
and reveal God.
All of Creation is essentially Good.

God dwells with us on earth,
animating and transforming everything
making all of Creation
Sacramental.

I believe that
Humans, as created beings,
are designed for a Noble End.
Human Life is precious.

Our Life Journey is fraught with meaning.

With Free Will to accept or reject
The Noble Challenge to a High and
Dignified Calling,
Human Life is intensely dramatic.
Our struggles are significant.

My Faith is Optimistic.

Where there is Life, there is Hope.

No matter how tragic are life's events,
my Faith rejects despair.

I am always hopeful.

My Faith does not take me
out of the world,
but ever deeper into it.

My Faith
Is steeped in Mystery
and an intense Delight in Creation.

My Faith
is lofty while sensual,
and
Heaven-directed while earthbound.

Human Life on earth is Mystery,

an intersection of the Natural and

Supernatural.

Theology and Dialogue

Connection and Dialogue,
so fundamental to Christianity,
(Jesus was constantly in Dialogue with
Others)
is strangely missing in today's Catholicism.

Theology is born through Questions
that are asked by contemporaries and
one must start by Listening
before proclaiming summaries of long ago.

The Quest for Truth pre-supposes Dialogue.

The tentative Dialogue of Vatican II
did not last long.
And the poor dialogue has resulted in
poor theology.

We see this with the present hierarchy
where the paramount concern is
preservation of the institution,
A theological crisis!

The bad theology we oft hear on Sundays
compounds the problem.

We have had bold and prophetic
theologians
Who re-think and re-formulate Faith
for today and tomorrow,
but they have paid a high price:
threatened, sacked, exiled, silenced.

We have bad theology because of
the ruling structures of the church,
who take little account of theologians
and make a narrow orthodoxy
the measure of loyalty.

They confuse thirst
with relativism
and continue to launch anathemas,
forbidding new thoughts of
the poetry of theological work.

Good theology,
the basis of a healthy church,
is humans taking hold of
the Word of God,
kneading it,
shaping it into human words and images,
baking it in the fire of critical dialogue,
so that it can be received as
the bread of life
by ALL God's people.

Good Theology cannot be
the voice of only one group
of the human family,
as it needs the full range of human
experience,
including the voice of
the poor and rich,
females and males,
lay people and ordained,
Catholics and not.